# JEDIDIAH

"Loved by the Lord"

Copyright © 2018 by Steven D. Cole
ISBN 978-1-7241-2921-5

All rights reserved. No part of this book may be reproduced or used in any manner without written permission of the copyright owner, except for the use of quotations in a book review.

"…and because the Lord loved him, he sent word through Nathan the prophet to name him Jedidiah."

— 2 Samuel 12:25 (NIV)

# Table of Contents

Preface .................................................................................... 1
1 Jedidiah ............................................................................. 3
2 A Taste of Something Better ........................................... 7
3 Separation Anxiety ........................................................ 11
4 Laughter ......................................................................... 15
5 Giving Paw .................................................................... 19
6 Finding Our Calling ...................................................... 23
7 Dependence ................................................................... 27
8 Loving Dog and God .................................................... 31
9 Delighting in Mercy ...................................................... 35
10 Distractions ................................................................... 39
11 Submission .................................................................... 43
12 Pleasure in One Another's Presence ............................ 47
13 Unconditional Love, Part I ........................................... 51
14 Unconditional Love, Part II .......................................... 55
15 Out of Control ............................................................... 59
16 Saying Thanks ............................................................... 63
17 Comprehension ............................................................. 67
18 Naughtiness ................................................................... 71
19 Others Just Don't Understand ...................................... 75
20 Sense of Time ................................................................ 79
21 Ticks ............................................................................... 83
22 Hiding Our Emotions ................................................... 87
23 Friendship ..................................................................... 91
24 Complaining .................................................................. 95

| | | |
|---|---|---|
| 25 | Treats | 99 |
| 26 | Fence Gates | 103 |
| 27 | Discontentment | 107 |
| 28 | Loved by the Lord | 111 |
| 29 | Healing | 115 |
| 30 | Obedience Training | 119 |
| 31 | The Call of the Wild | 123 |
| 32 | Take a Walk | 127 |
| 33 | Behind the Scenes | 131 |
| 34 | My Muddy Buddy | 135 |
| 35 | Self-Centeredness | 139 |
| 36 | Trusting | 143 |
| 37 | At Our Worst | 147 |
| 38 | Gifts | 151 |
| 39 | Being Muzzled | 155 |
| 40 | In the Storm | 159 |
| 41 | Joy | 163 |
| 42 | Getting Worked Up Over the Littlest Things | 167 |
| 43 | Saying No | 171 |
| 44 | Learning to Heel | 175 |
| 45 | Plastic Packaging | 179 |
| 46 | Pride | 183 |
| 47 | Waiting | 187 |
| 48 | Appreciation | 191 |
| 49 | The Walk and the Journey | 195 |
| 50 | Bragging | 199 |
| | About the Author | 205 |

# Preface

The name "Jedidiah" is used just once in Scripture. Though it refers to Solomon, its meaning, "loved by the Lord," applies to all of us. John wrote that God, "loved us and sent his Son as an atoning sacrifice for our sins." (1 John 4:10, NIV) And, famously, the Gospel writer penned these words: "For God so loved the world that he gave his only Son, so that everyone who believes in him may not perish but may have eternal life." (John 3:16, NRSV) Have no doubt that if you believe in Jesus, you too are the Lord's beloved.

Five years into our marriage, my wife and I felt that the time was right for us to adopt a puppy, so we chose to add an Alaskan Malamute to our family. We selected this breed because they are regal and beautiful and are known to be both very affectionate and stubborn. Their personalities are as big as their stature. And we have found this to be true with our beloved Malamute, to whom we fittingly gave the name "Jedidiah," for we believe that he too is very much loved by the Lord. For more than ten years, Jedidiah has been our "adogable" companion whom God has used to serve as an inspiration for this book.

If you are reading this, I feel safe in presuming that you are a follower of Jesus and also that you have at least one special, four-legged companion who has stolen your heart. And you may have observed that there are some very interesting parallels with regard to people's love for their dogs and God's love for us, His children. And vice versa. As God loves us, so do we love our dogs. As God disciplines us, so do we discipline our dogs. As our dogs ought to trust us, so ought we to trust God. And so forth.

This book draws upon these themes, as well as personal anecdotes involving Jedidiah, to illustrate these truths. It consists of fifty devotional readings, each with an accompanying verse of Scripture for meditation, four to six questions for self-reflection, and a prayer. I encourage you to write down your responses to the questions, rather than quickly glossing over them in your mind. I also encourage you to make the prayers your own by praying them out loud, and adding whatever is on your heart. And I highly recommend that you set aside a time and choose a place free of distraction for each devotional reading.

The heart behind this book is to enable you to experience intimate communion with the Father as you read, reflect, and pray in His presence. My hope and prayer is that you will smile, be challenged, be encouraged, and grow in appreciation for the love and care that God has uniquely for you.

*Please note that the male pronoun has been used throughout this book when referring to one's dog. This is done simply in order to eliminate unnecessary wordiness in the passages. No bias or offense is intended.*

# 1 Jedidiah

The story of David and Bathsheba is a tragic one indeed. Mighty, faithful King David, "a man after God's own heart," falls to the sins of the flesh by committing adultery with a married woman, resulting in her becoming pregnant. He tries to cover it up, and falls further, indirectly ordering the murder of Bathsheba's righteous husband, Uriah. David is then confronted by his close friend, the prophet Nathan, who brings his sin to light. David confesses and is heartbroken, and Nathan declares the Lord's forgiveness. Nevertheless, the consequence of David's showing contempt for the Lord is that the child that Bathsheba bore to David will not survive. Thereafter, the child becomes ill and, despite seven days of David fasting and pleading to God, the child dies.

David accepts the result, acknowledging that the death of another innocent life is on his head. He then goes to Bathsheba to comfort her, now his wife. But the story doesn't end there. This is a God story, and God stories almost always involve human failings and godly redemption. To "redeem" means to be delivered from some evil by the paying of a price. And in this story, redemption begins with the birth of another child to David and Bathsheba. Picking up the biblical narrative, we read, "…and they named him Solomon. The Lord loved him; and because the Lord loved him, he sent word through Nathan the prophet to name him Jedidiah." (2 Samuel 12:24-25, NIV)

Most study Bibles have a footnote at the end of verse 25, explaining that "Jedidiah" means "loved by the Lord" or "the Lord's beloved." For reasons unknown, the biblical authors use the name "Solomon" henceforth in the narrative; the name "Jedidiah" is mentioned just this one time in all of Scripture. But there is reason to pause and meditate on this name for a bit.

Jedidiah.

Loved by the Lord.

The Lord's beloved.

This was God's promise to David, delivered through the same prophet who brought to David the devastating news that his first child with Bathsheba would be stricken and die. But this latter message was that this child would be blessed. This child was loved by the Lord. It was God's way of saying, "David, your sin is not being held against you. I have separated it from you as far as the east is from the west." It is a beautiful act of redemption—that David's relationship with Bathsheba, which had begun in an unimaginably offensive fashion, could be redeemed by a loving and forgiving God.

Fast forward about a thousand years, and then comes the cross of Christ. And the resurrection. God's redemption of all humanity. On the cross, Jesus took upon Himself the sins of the world, paying the death penalty that we all deserve and forever removing from us the consequences of our sin, for all who accept this gift of grace. Now, in Christ, there is the undeniable promise not only of God's forgiveness, but also of God's love. In Christ, you too are declared to be God's beloved. You are, in a very real sense, "Jedidiah." You are indeed loved by the Lord.

In 2007, my wife and I were in our fifth year of marriage and we knew that it was time to extend our family of two to a family of three. We were united in our desire to adopt a puppy that would grow into a big, cuddly dog. One that we could wrap our arms around and by which we could be enveloped. We also wanted a dog with a personality. Secretly, I was also okay with a little stubbornness. After much research, we discovered the most noble, beautiful, rewarding breed of dog on the planet (in this author's opinion), the Alaskan Malamute. And so we adopted an uber-cute but strong-headed little puppy to whom we gave the name "Jedidiah." For he too, we believe, is loved by the Lord.

> "Then David consoled his wife Bathsheba, and went to her, and lay with her; and she bore a son, and he named him Solomon. The Lord loved him, and sent a message by the prophet Nathan; so he named him Jedidiah, because of the Lord."
> — 2 Samuel 12:24-25 (NRSV)

- In your own words, what does it mean to be loved by the Lord?

- Do you truly believe that you are the Lord's beloved? Do you believe it on an intellectual level? Do you feel it on an emotional level as well?

- Think about how much you love your dog. Can you imagine God loving you in the same way? Even more so?

- If there is any doubt in your mind or your heart as to God's perfect love for you, what is causing that doubt?

- What would you need to hear from God to be convinced of, or feel, His love for you?

*Dear Lord, being called "Jedidiah" is overwhelming. I am Your beloved? Really? Help me to internalize that, please. You and I both know my many shortcomings and imperfections. But then again, I really do love my dog. And we both know that he isn't perfect, by any means. But despite that, I still love him. I do. So maybe that is kind of how You feel about me? I know I'm not that cute, but You really do love me that much? Wow. It might take some time for me to grasp that, but I guess that a God who created puppies must be capable of incredible, beautiful love. I love You, Lord. Take me deeper, I pray. In Jesus' name. Amen.*

# 2 A Taste of Something Better

Maybe your dog is a picky eater. Or maybe your dog eats everything in sight. But even the hungriest dog with the most wolfish of appetites will leave his bowl of kibble behind and come scampering into the kitchen when he hears the unwrapping of a plastic bag or other container that is likely to hold, as its contents, the greatest treat a dog can imagine—people food!

When I was younger, dreaming of someday being a proud dog owner, I recall saying to a friend of mine, "When I am fortunate enough to have a dog of my own, he's never getting any people food. I don't want him to be picky, so I will feed him only kibble and dog treats so that he will never know the taste of people food and refuse to eat his dog food." A few years ago, after that same friend witnessed me letting Jedidiah lick my dinner plate before placing it in the dishwasher, he reminded me of what I had once said to him. Oh well, I guess my convictions weren't quite as strong as I had thought.

You see, I wanted to teach my dog contentment. If he didn't know anything other than dry dog food, he'd be happy with it and wouldn't desire more tasty, people food. Or so I thought. But eventually I broke down and gave in to satisfying his curiosity to taste what he could surely smell in our kitchen. At that point, he must have realized that what he had been eating all along—although very high quality dog food—was only a taste of the endless possibilities of flavors which could entice and satisfy his taste buds. Simply put: *he desired more.*

Certain Eastern philosophies teach that desire is a bad thing. They believe that desire leads to unfulfillment, which in turn leads to suffering. To avoid suffering, it is taught that desire must be squashed. But such is not the case in Christ's teachings. He generally appealed to people's desires in order to shift the focus of their hearts toward God. Jesus often asked, "What do you want?" or, "What do you want Me to do for you?" in order to help people identify their true desires and voice these needs to God.

Just as eating people food opens a dog's eyes to a world of possibilities of palatable sensation, sometimes we too get a "taste" of something deep, meaningful, and true, and it awakens our senses to the fact that there is something greater out there. There is a God and all His wonderful marvels, and there is a heaven that awaits us beyond this earthly life. Sometimes we experience that taste in the beauty of nature. Sometimes it's the compassion of another. Sometimes it's a story in a movie that stirs something deep within us that makes us want to jump up and shout, "Yes, there's more to life than this and I want to live it to the full!"

*Desire.* When that part of our heart is awakened, we realize that there is more to our existence than what we can see with our eyes and taste with our mouths. In his letter to the church in Philippi, Paul wrote about the value of contentment, sure, but he also wrote about pressing on, "for the prize of the heavenly call of God in Christ Jesus." (Philippians 3:14, NRSV) In other words, don't quit training for the 10K that you've always wanted to run. Don't be satisfied with chuck roast when filet mignon is being offered. Don't choose to play nine holes at your local golf course if someone is offering to take you to Pebble Beach. *There's more.*

These moments of realizing that there is indeed more are windows into heaven. Taste and savor their goodness. And as you love seeing the satisfaction that a bite of people food gives to your dog, imagine how God smiles down upon you as you savor these moments. I challenge you: *dare to desire.*

**"As the deer pants for streams of water, so my soul pants for you, my God." — Psalm 42:1 (NIV)**

- On a scale of 1 to 10, how much would you say that your dog craves people food?

- How often does your dog get a taste of yummy people food from your kitchen?

- What can we learn from our dogs here? If they unabashedly desire and ask for the tastiest snacks, shouldn't we in the same manner crave God and the blessings of heaven?

- What is it that you truly desire?

- Do you believe that all of your desires will find fulfillment in heaven?

*Dear Lord, thank You for the many lessons that You teach me through my dog. Even a nuisance behavior such as begging for table scraps can hold profound meaning. Just as my dog unabashedly asks for people food, please fan the flame within my soul that longs for goodness and holiness in my life. Help me to desire Your presence and to savor those moments when heaven feels oh so close. In Jesus' name. Amen.*

# 3 Separation Anxiety

Many dog owners have a special part of the house where they confine their pet when they leave home. For some, it might be the laundry room or the basement. For others, it might be the sunroom or the kitchen. Over time, the dog may learn to get used to the confinement when his master is away, but can you recall what it was like the first few times you embarked upon this little endeavor? No doubt little Snoopy or Rex was not too happy. And I don't think it was really the confinement that sent him into a state of deep worry. No, more likely it was the fact that a barrier now separated the little one from his loving master. And once you left the house, perhaps you heard the blood-curdling wails and cries coming from inside the house. Translation: "Woe is me! My master has left me all alone and I don't know when he's coming back!"

Separation anxiety. It's that state of nervousness and overall unrest experienced when we cannot be with the one we love. This inner turmoil is not unique to dogs, of course. It is commonly experienced by teenagers who leave home for the first time to attend college, or by young lovers who find themselves drawn apart by many miles. But it is also experienced at times by Christians when they feel the agony of separation from their loving Master.

"Separation from God?" you might ask. True, the Lord has said that He will never leave you nor forsake you. (Hebrews 13:5) But there are times when it feels as though the separation is palpable. And this usually occurs following sin. Sin is deliberately putting our own self-centered wants ahead of what we know God desires for us. And though forgiveness is available when we repent, that sin has the effect of building what seems like a brick wall between us and God. We feel as though we cannot ask Him for anything in prayer since there exists a heavy burden on our hearts—a feeling that we have disappointed Him by indulging in disobedience. We feel that we have no right to experience His blessings because of what we have done. In these times, true repentance in the form of a broken and contrite heart is the only remedy that is effective at breaking down that wall and restoring our communion with the Father.

Jesus experienced this separation anxiety on the cross. Hanging there, condemned to death, Jesus took upon Himself the sin of the entire world. It was at that moment that the Son experienced the anguish of having the Father's face turned from Him. It was then when He cried out, "Eloi, Eloi, lema sabachthani?" which means, "My God, my God, why have you forsaken me?" (Mark 15:34, NRSV) In this anguished cry, Jesus both (i) expressed that all-too-real pain of separation from God the Father, and also (ii) alluded to Psalm 22, which prophetically foretold the death to be suffered by the Messiah. Yes, God knows well the pain of separation anxiety.

Just as it probably pains your heart to hear your little fluffball whining and crying as you leave him locked up at home, I think it must pain God as well when we sin and build that wall between us, disrupting the free-flowing communion that we ordinarily experience with Him on a daily basis. But then, think about the moment of joy experienced when you come home from running your errands, open the door, and free your little one from his jail cell. Tails are wagging, tongues are hanging out, there's jumping and embracing and rejoicing. What a moment! So, the next time that you stumble and allow sin to come into your life and disrupt your relationship with your heavenly Father, don't hesitate in coming to Him in prayer and repentance, so that He might experience your heart-felt devotion and you might feel His loving arms again, and rejoice in that moment of reconciliation.

> "I am not sorry that I sent that severe letter to you, though I was sorry at first, for I know it was painful to you for a little while. Now I am glad I sent it, not because it hurt you, but because the pain caused you to repent and change your ways. It was the kind of sorrow God wants his people to have, so you were not harmed by us in any way."
> — 2 Corinthians 7:8-9 (NLT)

- Is there a place in your home—a room or a crate—where you confine your dog when you are gone?

- How did your dog respond the first time you left him alone?

- After falling into sin, do you find the image of a brick wall being erected between you and God to be an appropriate one?

- Recall the last time you felt this separation anxiety, as though you were no longer in fellowship with God. How long did it last? What brought about an end to it?

- Think about how happy you are to return home and greet your dog. And how happy he is to see you. How do you think God feels when you return to Him in prayer after a time of separation?

*Dear Lord, I hate sin. I don't know why I do it. I experience pleasure but for a brief moment, but that is followed by a time of deep heartbreak and a feeling of separation from You. I always regret it. Every time. And then, in shame and sorrow, I come crawling back to You, asking for forgiveness and restoration. And You always welcome me back. Every time. Thank You for putting up with me. Help me to make more godly decisions in the future, starting right now. And thank You for the pain of separation anxiety, since it teaches me that my comfort and peace are only found in a right relationship with You. In Jesus' name. Amen.*

# 4 Laughter

Laughter is a wonderful thing. Who doesn't like to laugh? Where does laughter come from, anyway? Is there an evolutionary advantage to laughing? I'm really not sure, but it sure is refreshing.

In my experience, I've never known a dog to laugh, but I sure laugh at mine. A lot! I'm sure you laugh at your dog's silly antics as well. With Jedidiah, it can be almost anything. Lying down with his head nestled against a piece of furniture so that his neck arches all the way back, and seemingly finding that to be a comfortable position. Rolling a bowling ball across the carpet with his nose. Woo-wooing like crazy in the yard because he's stumbled across a turtle. Doing laps around the house because he wants to be chased. Or picking up and throwing his toys. Once at the dinner table, I had just finished eating, and Jed approached me with a plush lobster toy, and he tossed it up and it landed right onto my dinner plate! Seriously!

You know how parents tend to think that their kids are the cutest ones in the world? They proudly show you pictures and you politely "ooh" and "ahh" and make nice comments. Personally, I don't get it. When I see a picture of someone's baby, that's all I see—a baby. They all look kind of the same to me. But as dog owners, sometimes we fall into the same trap as well—that is, thinking that our dog is the cutest and best of them all. Perhaps we may acknowledge that, objectively, this might not be true. But then again, how could cuteness and "bestness" even be quantified or measured objectively? These are subjective terms, and maybe it's okay for every dog owner to believe in his or her heart that their pooch really is the best. It's really not about comparison; it's about compassion…and love.

So where does God come into all of this? Think about it for a minute. We are all His children. Each and every one of us is singularly loved and adored by God. We're all His favorites. Again, I'm not comparing. He just loves us all individually that much! And think of all the silly, dumb things we do. You know those times when we laugh at ourselves? Like a few months ago when I put on my wife's tee shirt, thinking it was mine. (We have identical, white tee shirts with a small picture of a Malamute on the chest, only mine is a large and hers is a medium.) It felt a bit tight when I put it on, but I just concluded that the weight-lifting I had been doing lately was really starting to have a noticeable effect! Oh brother. You know what, though? I can't hide anything from God, and I bet He chuckled at that. I bet God laughs along with us at our silly antics all the time. After all, He created us in order to enjoy a relationship with us, right? And what is more enjoyable in a relationship than the ability to laugh with one another?

God must have a great sense of humor. If you recall, the people flocked to Jesus. And though His teaching must have been remarkable, I'm sure it was more than this that made Him so attractive, because it wasn't just those people who were looking for religious instruction that stuck by His side. Jesus was accused of being a sinner and a drunkard because of the company He kept. Now, think about it for a minute. What types of sounds are associated with these kinds of rabble-rousers? I imagine the clinking of beer mugs together and a whole lot of raucous laughter. Yes, Jesus really must have been the life of the party to have gathered such a crowd! I'm sure His laughter was contagious as well. It's no wonder that German theologian Meister Eckhart (1260-1328 A.D.) famously wrote that, "we are born out of the laughter of the Trinity."

So the next time you see your dog doing something that just tickles you, laugh it up. Revel in it. And then when you find yourself being a goofball or doing something extra silly, like scouring the house to find your phone when you're unknowingly carrying it around in your pocket the whole time, laugh at yourself, and know that God is laughing alongside you.

**"You have turned my mourning into joyful dancing. You have taken away my clothes of mourning and clothed me with joy, that I might sing praises to you and not be silent. O Lord my God, I will give you thanks forever!"** — Psalm 30:11-12 (NLT)

- What was the last occasion you had to laugh at (or with) your dog?

- Reflect upon how much joy it brings you to laugh in the presence of your dog. Isn't that one of the best benefits of having a canine companion?

- What types of things do you think God finds humorous?

- Can you think of any stories recorded in the Bible that are just plain funny?

- What is one silly thing that you did in the past seven days that you think is something God would have laughed at?

*Dear Lord, thank You for laughter. I'm not sure if I've ever prayed that prayer before. I've thanked You for life and breath and health and sunsets and great food and my dog. But thank You, really, for laughter. Thank You for the antics of my dog, which make me chuckle and smile, and the light he brings to my life each day. I hope, Lord, that You can take delight in the silly, dumb things I sometimes do. So when I'm tempted to get mad at myself for being stupid, please remind me that it's just silliness and that You're laughing alongside me. In Jesus' name. Amen.*

# 5 Giving Paw

Isn't it funny how we all tend to teach our dogs to sit and give us their paw, and we reward them with a treat? We're so proud of them when they learn to do this. And then when we're eating something that they want, they sit down and give us their paw, expecting to get the food we're eating. How do we then go about explaining to them, "This only works when I tell you to sit and I ask for your paw. You can't just give me your paw anytime you want the food I have in my hand." Honestly, I can understand the dog's confusion: "You taught me that if I sit and give you my paw, I get a treat. Now you're changing the rules? Not fair!"

Like most dogs, Jedidiah has learned that "paw" usually equals "treat." And he's also learned that when he puts his chin down on the edge of the couch or the ottoman, I respond with a look and an "awww" indicating how pleased I am, because it's just so darn cute. And if I'm eating something at the time, I usually give him a bite. So now when I want to have a snack while sitting on the couch, such as popcorn, I have to put a small towel down on the cushion next to me in order to catch his drool as he chews on bite after bite of popcorn. It really is too cute to resist. But the fabric does not take too kindly to his slobber.

In addition to breakfast and dinner, Jed always gets a treat (a rubber toy stuffed with food) at precisely 2:00 p.m. And when I forget, he'll come and stick his nose in my elbow or stare me down, and I'll look at my watch and see that it's often exactly two o'clock to the minute. But sometimes he gets antsy and starts bugging me early. This happened recently, as I was trying to pray. I was sitting with my eyes closed at around one o'clock, and my arms kept getting raked by his nails. Jed was giving me paw over and over again. "I want my treat, Daddy!" After trying unsuccessfully to ignore it, I stopped, rubbed his chest, and asked him to be patient and wait for the right time.

As I closed my eyes again, still rubbing Jed's chest, I began to think about how often I am like this with God. I am asking for blessings and answered prayers now, in my timing. I'm essentially giving God my paw so that He'll give me what I want right now. I don't think we're really pestering God when we come to Him in prayer over and over. Jesus taught His disciples to "keep on praying" to the Father, of course. But we mustn't demand His answer right away. Faith means believing and hoping for what we cannot see. We might not be able to hear God saying, "Yes, child, I hear your prayer," but we must exercise the faith to believe that He does. And maybe His answer is going to be, "No," because He knows that to answer the prayer the way we want Him to is not going to be very good for us. And maybe His answer is going to be, "Yes, but not just yet," because He's already worked out the answer in a beautiful way, but it will take time for everything to fall into place. We must trust that God hears our prayers, we must trust that He is always providing His best for us, and we must always trust His timing.

Sometimes there is more going on behind the scenes of which we're unaware. Think of Daniel's prayers going unanswered for three weeks because the angel who showed up to answer him had been delayed by some sort of spiritual warfare. (Daniel 10:12-14) Or the story of Elisha's servant being given, for a moment, the ability to see horses and chariots of fire in the spiritual realm that were there to protect him and Elisha. (2 Kings 6:15-17) And sometimes we're just not ready for that prayer to be answered, because God is still working on changing us on the inside. For instance, we might be praying for God's vocational calling to be revealed in our life, but God knows that much more heart change is required before we can step into that destiny.

So let's continue to pray, believing that God is hearing every spoken word and every unspoken heart's desire that we bring before Him. And let's believe that we're to expect great things from God, but let's also be patient as we extend our paw to Him, realizing that His timing is always best.

> "Do not lag in zeal, be ardent in spirit, serve the Lord.
> Rejoice in hope, be patient in suffering, persevere in prayer."
> — Romans 12:11-12 (NRSV)

- Does your dog sit and give you his paw when you ask it of him?

- Does your dog sit and give you his paw when you are eating something tasty, and are not asking for his paw?

- When your dog wants something from you, what does he typically do to let you know?

- What prayers have you prayed that you wanted God to answer right away, but He didn't?

- Looking back, are there prayers that God did answer, but only much later?

- What prayers are you praying to be answered right now? Do you believe that God is hearing you, and that He might be waiting for a certain time to show You the answer?

*Dear Lord, my tendency, like that of my dog, is to ask for the things I want to be delivered to me instantaneously. These include prayers for provision, for blessing, for healing, and for the salvation of loved ones. I believe that You are honored when I keep on praying for these things, and I will commit to always bringing these prayer requests before You. You are my provision for everything. But help me to trust You with the answers. I believe that You hear my prayers, and I acknowledge that I don't know why I sometimes don't see the answers in the timing or the manner in which I want. But I trust in Your goodness and Your timing. Please increase my faith. In Jesus' name. Amen.*

# 6 Finding Our Calling

Dogs are wonderfully diverse. There are large, muscular dogs. There are little, yappy dogs. There are sleepy, lazy dogs. Some like to wander off and explore. Others never leave their master's side. Some are super cute. Some are intimidating. Some seem to be smiling all the time. And some look as though they are always grouchy. You get the picture.

While we mostly think of dogs as pets nowadays, different breeds were developed in order to do certain chores for people. For instance, certain breeds fall into the category of "herding dogs" and have been put to work moving herds of cattle or sheep. Interestingly, some breeds of herders, such as the Australian Cattle Dog, do so by nipping at the heels of animals to move the herd in a certain direction. Others, like the Border Collie, get in front of the animals and stare them down, thus altering their direction with intimidation.

Herding dogs are just one category, of course. There are numerous breeds that were bred to aid hunters. Retrievers and Spaniels, for instance, were bred to flush out and retrieve fowl. The Doberman Pinscher is one of several breeds that were developed primarily to guard both livestock and their owners. Siberian Huskies are famous for pulling sleds across the arctic tundra. And, of course, Pomeranians were bred to be carried around in little pink purses by upscale, urban housewives.

The point is that each breed has a purpose, or a "calling" if you will. It is in that dog's DNA. It's what makes him come alive. Our Alaskan Malamute, Jedidiah, was born in North Carolina, but he is a sled dog at heart. He loves the snow and he loves to pull. We don't get nearly enough snow in Virginia to satisfy his craving for the white manna from heaven, but even in the summertime there is still a chance for Jed to connect with his inner self. When I put his pulling harness on him and strap on my inline skates, by his reaction you'd think it was Christmas morning! Sometimes I've had to step outside to lace up my skates because Jed has been all over me, brimming with uncontrolled excitement. And then I hook up his leash and we hit the street and it feels to me like we're traveling at the speed of light. Well, we may not have ever actually broken the speed limit, but it sure is a rush for the both of us.

For a Malamute, pulling is what he was bred to do, and more than anything it's what makes him come alive. Perhaps you have a herding dog as a pet. My grandparents had a Shetland Sheepdog, and when we would go to visit as a family, Scottie would do all he could to make sure we were all in the same room together. He was herding us! Throw a ball for a Retriever. Again and again and again. It never gets old.

A dog doesn't have to agonize or pray about his calling in life. It's tied to his breed, and it flows naturally from within. Throughout my twenties, I spent many a frustrating hour agonizing over what God had called me to in life vocationally. Prayer after prayer seemed to go unanswered. And I know I'm not alone. I have spoken, counseled, and prayed with many young men and women that have been asking the same question: "God, what is my calling? What was I born to do in this life?"

I don't take this topic lightly because it has given me more grief than I care to admit. Perhaps the most helpful guidance I ever received on this topic is a quote attributed to philosopher, theologian, and civil rights leader Howard Thurman, who advised, "Don't ask what the world needs. Ask what makes you come alive, and go do it. Because what the world needs is people who have come alive." Your calling is not some secret plan that God has hidden from you, which you have to diligently seek out, like a lab rat running through a maze, trying to find the piece of cheese, with difficult make-it-or-break-it decisions at every intersection. Your calling becomes more and more clear as you seek to walk closer and closer with God and He shows you the desires that He has placed on your heart. Just as a Husky lives to pull and a Retriever lives to retrieve, there are godly desires within you that make you come alive. And pursuing those, while intimately walking alongside the Lord of the universe, is how you follow your calling.

> "Take delight in the Lord, and He will give you the desires of your heart. Commit your way to the Lord; trust in him, and he will act. He will make your vindication shine like the light, and the justice of your cause like the noonday."
> — **Psalm 37:4-6 (NRSV)**

- What type of work were your dog's ancestors bred to do?

- Do you find it true that your dog "comes alive" when he is doing something along these same lines?

- When was the last time you played with your dog in such a way as to enable him to enjoy his calling?

- How does it make you feel to see your dog enjoying himself like this?

- Pause for a minute and think about what makes you come alive. Don't feel pressured into giving some answer that would be vocationally relevant. Just be honest. You owe that to yourself and to God.

- If you take joy in seeing your dog come alive in some activity, how do you think God feels when you do what excites you?

*Dear Lord, sometimes I have a hard time connecting what makes me come alive with what I think You want me to do with my life. I have a hard time believing that my enjoyment would ever align with Your will, and that whatever calling You place on my life is something dreadful. Please forgive me for not trusting in the goodness of Your heart. I may not know what my "calling" in life is at this moment, but, if You're not going to reveal it to me supernaturally, please help me to at least not fear that it would be something distasteful, and to believe that it would align with what makes me come alive. Please walk me through these difficult questions as I continue to pursue intimacy and joy alongside You. In Jesus' name. Amen.*

# 7 Dependence

Something we may not think about all that much is just how utterly and completely dogs depend upon their owners to provide for their basic needs. Dogs don't have the ability to open the refrigerator, use a can opener, or fill their water bowl at the sink. Without us, they cannot get the basic sustenance they need to live. I suppose if we left a paper bag of kibble accessible and the toilet lid up, they could survive for a time… But it's not only food and water that they need, it's also shelter, so they can find refuge inside during the harsh cold of winter and those "dog days" of summer when the mercury just about bursts the thermometer. Even those nasty, uncomfortable visits to the vet ensure their health. A dog may be able to lick his wounds, but he cannot vaccinate himself or apply flea and tick preventatives.

These basic necessities are those things for which your dog has come to depend on you. You are his source of life-sustaining provision. He expects you to provide these things; indeed, he relies upon you to sustain his very life. He literally would die without your basic care. To be honest, your dog probably doesn't ponder these things when he's lying on his bed, lazing the day away. But if you were to leave for work and not return, you can bet he'd be in a panic.

In a similar vein, we too are totally dependent upon our heavenly Father to provide for our basic needs. He has provided us an atmosphere with just the right mixture of oxygen, nitrogen, and other gases so that we can breathe and not be asphyxiated. He has created plants and animals to nourish us. Without water, we would not last one week. He even enables us to sleep so that our bodies can get the rest and recovery needed to take on another day. And can I be honest? I think we all expect this of God. He fathers the entire human race by putting us in an environment in which our basic needs can be met, and He continues to supply these needs daily.

Have you ever had one of those times when you looked at your dog's water bowl and realized that it was empty? He must have been drinking more than usual that day and you didn't notice that it had gone dry. Or have you ever been out with your dog on a hike and forgot to bring water with you? Surely, you will search frantically for a stream or some other source of water so that he does not become dehydrated. How does that make you feel? Anxious? Worried? Like a lousy parent? Your puppster is relying on you for something as basic as water, and you've neglected to supply him with that need. At that time, you will do all you can as quickly as possible to meet that need once you have realized your mistake.

Thankfully, our God never forgets about us. He shepherds our hearts and draws us close to Him so that we might grow into mature adults, healing our wounds and straightening our character along the way. But He never stops caring for our basic needs. He never neglects us. He provides us with oxygen, food, water, and all the things upon which we are reliant to stay alive. From time to time, let us just acknowledge this fact and thank Him for ceaselessly supplying our daily, life-sustaining needs.

**"And my God will meet all your needs according to the riches of his glory in Christ Jesus. To our God and Father be glory for ever and ever. Amen." — Philippians 4:19-20 (NIV)**

- What are those basic needs that your dog has relied upon you to provide for him today?

- Do you think that your dog realizes how much he depends on you for these things?

- What life-sustaining needs has God provided for you today?

- What would happen if God "forgot" to supply just one of those things for you?

- When was the last time you felt unbearably hungry, thirsty, hot, cold, or tired? How did it make you feel?

- When did you last consciously take note of your reliance upon God for your every need?

*Dear Lord, You provide for my needs every day. You provide me with the breath of life, with food and drink and shelter and clothing. And sleep. Thank You for sleep! You care for me in such a loving manner and I confess that I rarely take notice of it. But I do now. In this moment, Lord, I thank You for providing for me. Thank You for giving me life and breath and all these things that I need in order to live. These are gracious gifts that You provide, and without them I would literally shrivel up and die. Thank You, Father, for calling me Your child and providing for me in this way. In Jesus' name. Amen.*

# 8 Loving Dog and God

I imagine that if you are reading this book, you would wholeheartedly say that you love God and that you love your dog. But let me ask you this: How do you show your dog that you love him? Surely you take care of him. You feed him, provide shelter for him, take him to the vet regularly for shots and check-ups. But aside from providing the basic necessities of life, I'm sure there's a lot more. I'm sure you pet him, snuggle, wrestle, take him for walks, go for rides in the car, play tug-of-war… If you're a loving dog owner, I'm sure you do everything you can to make him happy. If you were to say, "I love my dog," but didn't do any of these things, people would rightly question whether you actually understood what love is.

Paul famously wrote about love in 1 Corinthians 13. Love is patient, kind, rejoices in the truth, believes, hopes, and endures all things, etc. But what is love without loving acts? You often hear the phrase "love in action," but can you tell me that there is really love without action? Especially when it comes to another person, or your dog, or God? If you say that you love your dog, but you do only the bare minimum to keep him alive, and do nothing to stimulate his senses or provide him with an outlet for play, or never pet, rub, or cuddle with him, are you really loving him? Because if you say that you love your dog but do none of these things, many would say that your words are meaningless.

The famous First Century leader of the Jerusalem Church, James, who is believed to be a half-brother of Jesus, wrote similarly about faith: "What good is it, my brothers and sisters, if you say you have faith but do not have works?" (James 2:14, NRSV) He goes on to write that just saying that you have faith in God, but not putting it into action by committing acts of love, is worthless: "So faith by itself, if it has no works, is dead." (James 2:17, NRSV) Ouch, James, that's harsh! But Jesus was never interested in lip-service Christianity, was He? He asked a lot of His followers. In fact, He asked everything of them. Take a look at this passage in Luke's Gospel:

> As they were going along the road, someone said to him, "I will follow you wherever you go." And Jesus said to him, "Foxes have holes, and birds of the air have nests; but the Son of Man has nowhere to lay his head." To another he said, "Follow me." But he said, "Lord, first let me go and bury my father." But Jesus said to him, "Let the dead bury their own dead; but as for you, go and proclaim the kingdom of God." Another said, "I will follow you, Lord; but let me first say farewell to those at my home." Jesus said to him, "No one who puts a hand to the plow and looks back is fit for the kingdom of God." (Luke 9:57-62, NRSV)

Matthew's Gospel records a parable told by Jesus, which presents a similar teaching:

> "What do you think? A man had two sons; he went to the first and said, 'Son, go and work in the vineyard today.' He answered, 'I will not'; but later he changed his mind and went. The father went to the second and said the same; and he answered, 'I go, sir'; but he did not go. Which of the two did the will of his father?" They [correctly] said, "The first." (Matthew 21:28-31, NRSV)

James and Jesus were both pretty clear—saying that you have faith, or love, without following through with action, demonstrates that you never really had the faith or love you claimed. I'm confident that your love for your dog motivates you to do things for him that make him happy. So I challenge you to demonstrate your love for God with acts of kindness and love as well.

> "If a brother or sister is naked and lacks daily food, and one of you says to them, 'Go in peace; keep warm and eat your fill,' and yet you do not supply their bodily needs, what is the good of that?" — James 2:15-16 (NRSV)

- What acts of love do you regularly perform for your dog that make him happy?

- How many acts of love have you performed for your dog over the past week?

- How many acts of love have you performed for another person over the past week?

- Do you see how James connects faith in God with performing acts of service?

- James gave an example in the above verses of what it means to show works of faith and love. Is there a "brother or sister," or family member, or friend, or someone in your community or church that is in need? What can you do to help him or her as an act of love for your God?

*Dear Lord, maybe it's just me, but I find that loving my dog is easy. I just love him—it's so natural, so naturally I want to pet him and play with him and give him treats. I love You too, but I confess that I'm not always so quick to connect loving You with performing acts of Christian charity for others. Please spur me on to demonstrate my love for You, God, in this way. May the words of James be more than an abstract biblical teaching; may they penetrate my heart and motivate me to act. In Jesus' name. Amen.*

# 9 Delighting in Mercy

You know that look. The big, weepy eyes. The head hanging low. The tail between the legs. It's the universal canine expression that says, "I've been bad and I know it." Even when we first see the wet spot on the carpet or the chewed-up slipper, that look still has a way of disarming us. It is tough to forgive a person when he or she fails to repent or acknowledge one's wrongdoing, but when your dog gives you that look, your heart simply melts. All of a sudden, your thoughts go from, "My carpet is ruined!" to, "I can run the steam cleaner over that spot and nobody will ever know."

My dog has a peculiar habit that he exhibits when he knows that he has done something wrong. He apologizes. No, really, he does. He will walk up to me slowly, sit down, and give me not one paw, but two! Both front legs extended onto my thighs. It has the effect of totally disarming any anger I had within me as my heart melts before his mixed display of cuteness and repentance.

Forgiving people who have wronged us is usually a difficult thing to do. Sometimes we must force ourselves to forgive the other person, not because we feel like it, but because we want to be obedient to God's commands. Forgiving our dogs is different. It is easier, mostly because we truly love them and don't want to stay mad at them, since we are eager to restore that loving relationship. The same is true with God and us. Do you think that God delights in meting out wrath and discipline? Not at all.

In the prophet Micah's day, the Israelite people were far from obedient to God's commands. Though they were the most privileged among all the nations to have God's law revealed solely to them, the political and religious leaders were as corrupt as those of any other nation. Maybe worse. They were obsessed with wealth, power, and social status. Deceit and bribery were common among the rulers and judges, and Micah spoke out boldly against such practices. He prophesied that God's judgment would come upon them in order to lead the nation to repentance, but he also spoke of God's forgiving and compassionate nature: "Who is a God like you, who pardons sin and forgives the transgression of the remnant of his inheritance? You do not stay angry forever but delight to show mercy." (Micah 7:18, NIV)

Just as we look for occasion to pardon our dogs when they acknowledge their naughtiness, so too does God delight in showing us mercy. He does not hold a grudge against His disobedient children, nor does He forgive begrudgingly. Rather, He does what He deems necessary to help draw His people to repentance, and then He mercifully offers forgiveness to the penitent. Furthermore, God does not keep a list of the sins that we have committed, only to read them back to us and belittle us. No, Micah states of God, "You will cast all our sins into the depths of the sea." (Micah 7:19, NRSV)

In other words, when we have misbehaved, we should come before God with our heads held low and our tail between our legs (*i.e.*, a posture and attitude of true repentance), along with a desire and willingness to change our ways, and God will gladly offer us sweet forgiveness and wipe our slate clean. He delights in showing mercy. We should afford Him such delight when appropriate.

"If we say that we have no sin, we deceive ourselves,
and the truth is not in us. If we confess our sins,
he who is faithful and just will forgive us our sins
and cleanse us from all unrighteousness."
— 1 John 1:8-9 (NRSV)

- What does your dog typically do when he acknowledges his naughty behavior?

- How do you respond when your dog "apologizes," or at least demonstrates that he knows that he's done something wrong?

- Have you ever thought of God as actually taking delight in showing mercy?

- What is the proper attitude and posture we should have before God after we have acted wrongfully?

- Examine yourself deeply for a moment. Is there any unconfessed sin that you need to bring before God right now? If so, apologize and ask for forgiveness, allowing God to delight in showing mercy to you.

*Dear Lord, I can't help but not stay mad at my dog when he gives me those big, weepy eyes. Despite the stained carpet, the chewed-up slipper, or whatever it is, I know that he's sorry and my heart forgives him. It's amazing that You feel the same way with me, one who knows full well the difference between right and wrong, and yet still chooses the wrong oh so often. I'm so sorry for doing the wrong over the right and I ask You to please forgive me for this. I come before You, Father, asking for a restored relationship. Please pick me up and hold me in Your arms. Thank You for taking delight in showing mercy, because I know that I need a lot of it. And grant me the grace to forgive others when they have wronged me. In Jesus' name. Amen.*

## 10 Distractions

Distractions are becoming more and more common in our lives, aren't they? It used to be that if a friend or family member wanted to get in touch with you, they would call your house on the telephone, and you would have to pick up a ringing, corded instrument and say, "Hello?" not knowing who was on the other end of the line. And before the days of the telephone, people would have to "call on you" by stopping by your residence and knocking on your door. Nowadays, everyone has their smartphone on their person at all times. You can be texted or e-mailed or called or, well, whatever new technology is next! But even when the device is not buzzing or vibrating or playing an annoying snippet of some popular song, alerting you to give it your attention, you can still touch it to make it come alive, and browse the internet or play games. I don't think there are many of the millennial generation in America who cannot go thirty seconds without receiving some sort of stimulation from their phones. Waiting in line at a store, or at a red light, their first impulse is usually to grab their phone. Of all the helpful ways that these devices can improve our quality of living, providing constant distraction is, in my opinion, not one of them.

If we are truly seeking God—to be close to Him and to hear from Him—silence must be an integral part of the equation. Silence and solitude. Far away from distractions. I have heard many stories of people sensing the gentle whisper of God's voice in times of quiet reflection and prayer; I have not yet heard a single story of God speaking to someone directly through a text message.

"But we lead such busy lives," you may counter. "How can I keep from being distracted all the time?" One way is to practice. If you start an exercise program, you begin by lifting smaller weights, and then build up over time as you get stronger. And for your cardio program, you don't start out by running five miles; it takes effort and discipline to build up to running longer distances. So start with five minutes of silence in the morning, just clearing your mind and asking God to be present with you. You can even set a timer on your smartphone! Then add a minute each day. While five minutes will seem like a really long time when you first try this, soon ten minutes will go by like the snap of a finger.

Another cure for distractions is to selectively embrace them. What I mean by that is…well, let's say you live near the mountains. They've become commonplace because you see them every day. Next time, take a second to look as though you are seeing them for the first time. Be distracted by their beauty. Same thing with the ocean, or a lake. Or the stars at night, which shine especially bright during a new moon. God's creation, untainted by human interference, is awe-inspiring when you take the time to appreciate it.

I had let Jedidiah outside one cool, early spring morning, and after wandering the yard, sniffing every bush and tree, he returned to the deck. But instead of coming right to the door to be let in, he laid down and rested his head on the horizontal two-by-four that makes up the lower part of the railing. Then he just gazed outward into the woods, conical ears moving like satellite dishes, picking up the sounds of birds and squirrels and who knows what else. He was distracted by the beauty of nature. And as I stood there, inside the door, watching him, guess what? I was distracted by the beauty of this large, magnificent dog lying on my deck, snout resting on the wood, enjoying the tranquility of the morning. And as my heart melted, I came to realize that I can choose to be distracted by e-mails, texts, and various other busy-body stuff, and I can let them affect my mood throughout the day. Or I can choose to take in the view of the Blue Ridge Mountains that I am privileged to have from my deck; or the stillness of the woods, interrupted only by a squirrel or two scurrying around on the fallen logs; or the bats fluttering around above the tree tops just before a summer sunset; or the breathtakingly beautiful dog who I get to love and father each and every day. Yes, we can *choose* to be distracted by beauty.

"The heavens declare the glory of God; the skies proclaim the work of his hands. Day after day they pour forth speech; night after night they reveal knowledge." — Psalm 19:1-2 (NIV)

- What are some of the common distractions that you face every day?

- How many times per day, or, dare I ask, per hour, are you distracted by your smartphone?

- What are the elements of nature close to your home that you see every day, but that you can choose to take a minute and gaze upon as if you were seeing them for the first time?

- What lessons can you learn from your dog about taking time to be silent in solitude?

- When was the last time you were taken aback by either the beauty of your dog, or the fact that you get to parent and love him every day?

- What can you do this week to intentionally spend quiet times with God and/or be distracted by beauty?

*Dear Lord, I sometimes feel assaulted by the texts, by the e-mails, by the phone calls, and everything else that tries to vie for my attention. And I confess that I contribute to it as well by not being content to be still and silent, but always wanting to fill those times with stimuli, whether it be through my smartphone or computer or TV or some other device. Please help me to make a resolution to slow down and be more intentional about spending times in the quiet, alone, just reflecting on You. And pouring my heart out to You. And help me, throughout the day, to be distracted by the beauty of nature around me. And that includes the beauty of my dog, for whom I thank You. In Jesus' name. Amen.*

# 11 Submission

When it is time to take Jedidiah for a walk, we have a harness that we put on him. It goes over his head, and then he steps through one part of it with his front-left paw, and then I connect it together on his right side with a plastic clip. I attach the leash to the harness, rather than to his collar, so that his neck doesn't get choked when he pulls. Jed knows what it means when he sees the harness—he's going out! Either for a walk or for a ride in the car. Either way, it's an exciting time. But he plays this funny game every time I pull out the harness, in which he tries to run away from me and I have to chase him around the house to catch him. He has an advantage on the carpeted surfaces, where he can get good traction, move quickly, and make sharp turns. The hardwood floors, though, are my territory. His paws don't grip so well, so he ends up running and running and getting nowhere, like Scooby Doo trying to run from a ghost. But when I do catch him, and it's time to put on the harness, Jed knows what to do. He doesn't fight it. He obediently puts his head down so that I can slide the harness over it, and then he lets me lift up the one paw, and stays still until he hears the "clippy thing" make its noise. In a word, he submits.

When Jesus told His disciples to take His yoke upon them, he was alluding to the practice of Middle Eastern agriculturists placing a wooden beam upon two oxen to join them together, so that they might share the load in pulling the plow. To be yoked, the oxen would have to stay still and lower their heads submissively. Jesus' invitation to His disciples was a gracious offer to come alongside them and share the load they were bearing. But to be yoked, or to be harnessed, requires a submissive posture. In order to accept Jesus' offer, we need to be still and, as some say, "lean into Jesus." This is not primarily about our physical posture (although being still and bowing our heads during prayer is certainly indicative of our submission to God); it is primarily about the attitude of our hearts. Submitting to Jesus' lordship. Allowing Him to carry our burdens. Intentionally praying that He might shoulder our cares and anxieties and the things weighing us down. He will respond; He has promised to do just that. And when we do submit, the burden becomes light.

Two oxen share the burden of pulling the plow; as they walk in step beside one another, the chore is much more manageable. Jed's harness is safer and more comfortable than if his leash were attached directly to his collar. It enables him to use his strong muscles to pull, without choking his neck. Likewise, walking through life with Jesus alongside us is a lot safer and more comfortable when we take a submissive posture, pray that we might be yoked to Him, and allow Jesus to share our burdens.

**"Come to me, all you that are weary and are carrying heavy burdens, and I will give you rest. Take my yoke upon you, and learn from me; for I am gentle and humble in heart, and you will find rest for your souls. For my yoke is easy, and my burden is light." — Matthew 11:28-30 (NRSV)**

- Do you use a harness to walk your dog? If so, does he submit when you put it on him?

- In general, is it better or worse for your dog when he submits to you?

- What cares, burdens, and anxieties are you carrying right now?

- Would you like Jesus to share the burden and give you rest?

- What can you do today to consciously yoke yourself to Jesus?

*Dear Lord, I shoulder a lot of burdens. I take on the burdens of [name them specifically]. Right now, I bow my head to You in a posture of submission and ask that we be yoked together. Thank You, Jesus, for Your offer to help me carry the load. I gratefully accept. Please help me to let go of the worries that do not help but only hinder my walk, and enable me to be joined with You in all that I have to do. And thank You for the peace and rest that You bring to me. I trust You alongside me. In Jesus' name. Amen.*

# 12 Pleasure in One Another's Presence

My dog loves being snuggled and petted. Belly rubs are his favorite, for sure. When he's lying on his side and I come over to him, that back leg automatically lifts up to reveal more of his underside. "Rub me here, Daddy." And I do, and he loves it. But what I like more is when he's sitting upright and regal, like a king, and I stroke his chest. His thick, white fur between my fingers. Up and down in a rhythmic manner. He stares straight ahead initially, but then his eyes roll back just a little, and his mouth opens, and his tongue sticks out a bit. And oh, it's a grand smile. Ecstasy. And it's contagious, for I am smiling like a happy dog myself. Chest rubs and smiles all around. It's a veritable lovefest.

I've often wondered what it is about being petted or rubbed that a dog likes so much. Is it the tactile sensation on his skin, or is it the intimacy shared with his loving master? I've come to conclude that it's both. The reason I think that is because, for me, it's also both. I love the way his plush fur feels against my hand. My favorite spot is the soft fur atop his head. It feels so good to rub my face in it. It really does. Like the feeling of a fleece blanket against one's skin. But it's more than that, because I don't get a giddy smile when I cover myself in a soft blanket. It's the intimacy—the love being shared. Innocent and kind. Love in its purest form, shared between human and canine.

It's almost cliché nowadays to hear in church that, "Christianity is not a religion, it's a relationship." Cliché or not, there is undeniable truth to that statement. God is not so much interested in our accomplishments as He is in our hearts. He didn't create worker bees to build nests; He created free-willed human beings in the hopes that we might voluntarily express back to Him love as He's shown to us. Relationship is about intimacy. If a man and his dog can find such loving warmth in the rubbing of one's fur, how much more can God and one of His beloved humans experience something similar, if not greater?

With my dog and me, it's primarily the chest rub where we share in the greatest intimacy. For you and your dog, maybe it's hugs or kisses or lying down beside one another or stroking him on your lap. It's personal. And it's the same way with God and each of us. Perhaps you feel that closest sense of intimacy with your heavenly Father when you're walking down a wooded trail, pondering His goodness and beauty and sharing your heart with Him out loud, where no one else can hear. Perhaps it's in the morning, with a cup of hot coffee and an open Bible. Perhaps it's at a worship service, with your hands and voice and spirit all lifted up in praise. He has created us all differently, and I think that God takes delight most when we express our love back to Him in the ways that come most naturally to us. Whatever the manner, these are precious, sacred moments, basked in by both us and God. Do not take them lightly, and do not neglect these times. Relationship is most holy during times of close, heart-felt intimacy. This is what God made you for. Love Him, and enjoy the peace and warmth that encompass these special moments.

> **"O God, you are my God, I seek you, my soul thirsts for you; my flesh faints for you, as in a dry and weary land where there is no water." — Psalm 63:1 (NRSV)**

- Where does your dog like most to be petted or rubbed?

- What is your favorite way of showing your dog how much you love him?

- At what times and in what ways do you feel most intimate with God?

- When is the last time you experienced this?

- Will you set aside some time this coming week, with no distractions, for nothing other than to worship God and let Him love on you?

*Dear Lord, I don't always feel that close to You, but there are times when I do feel as though I am exulting in Your love for me. And it is truly grand. It is in these times that I know what my dog must feel like when I am giving him a good rubbin'. Loved, truly and deeply loved. Thank You, Lord, for these times, and may I neither neglect them nor take them for granted. Call me closer, I pray, because I know that You enjoy these times as well, and I want to make sure that I never stop prioritizing the time I spend with You. It is life and joy and peace. And it is why I was made. In Jesus' name. Amen.*

# 13 Unconditional Love, Part I

If you were to survey one hundred dog owners and ask them, "What is the worst thing about having a dog?" I bet some of their responses would be scooping their poop, paying vet bills, and arranging for them to be taken care of when going on vacation. In fact, you would probably get a myriad of different answers amounting to quite a long list. So why do we even bother with all of the hassle of pet ownership…and do so voluntarily?

Two words: *Unconditional Love*.

Is there nothing so comforting and reassuring as knowing that when you come home at the end of a long, hard day that your canine companion will be eagerly waiting, with tail in full wag mode, sporting a big, goofy grin? "You're home! Let playtime commence!" Dogs are built to love. Even when you take away their toys, run the vacuum, and withhold those yummy table scraps, your dog still loves you. Your dog's love for you is not based on what you can do for him; it is pure, true, beautiful love—just because you are you. It is unconditional.

But is that how we love God? Or is the unspoken attitude of our hearts more along the lines of, "Lord, I will love You, but only if You do this, this, and this, and also keep this from ever happening to me?" Be honest with yourself. Do we love God because He is deserving of it, or is it conditioned upon how we perceive Him to be treating us?

Our love for God ought to be without condition—we are to love Him simply for who He is. He is God. He is perfect and holy. His very being is love. (1 John 4:8,16) Job is the biblical model of what it looks like to love God unconditionally. Even after all his property was destroyed, his children were killed, and his health was deteriorating, still Job proclaimed, "Blessed be the name of the Lord." (Job 1:21, NRSV)

I hope that none of us ever experience even a small portion of the catastrophic events that plagued Job. In the midst of our own circumstances, however, our posture toward God ought to be more like the loving devotion displayed to us by our dogs. Knowing that God is perfect, with only our best interests at heart, we are free to love Him unconditionally. Because He is God. Any condition to our love for Him—that is, if our love for God is based on anything other than who He is—is simply a matter of our failed perception of His true nature. It is the very character and nature of God—who God *is*—that invites our love...our unconditional love.

> "I will praise you, Lord, with all my heart; I will tell
> of all the marvelous things you have done.
> I will be filled with joy because of you.
> I will sing praises to your name, O Most High."
> — Psalm 9:1-2 (NLT)

- If surveyed, what would you say is the worst thing about having a dog?



- What about your dog makes you most glad?

- Would you even hesitate if you were asked whether you love your dog unconditionally?

- What conditions do we place upon God that we think He must fulfill in order that we may give Him our love and devotion?

- If these conditions were not met—if everything that could go wrong in your life all of a sudden went wrong—would you still love God? How would you respond in prayer?

*Dear Lord, please forgive me for basing my love and devotion for You on what You have provided for me. I do thank You for all these blessings. I am very grateful for them. But You deserve my love not because of anything You have done for me, but because of who You are. You are God. You are perfect. You are the very embodiment of love. Please purge me of the conditions I have placed on You. May my love for You be true, heartfelt, and unconditional. You deserve no less. In Jesus' name. Amen.*

# 14 Unconditional Love, Part II

Why do I love my dog?
Is it because he makes me smile? "Yes."
Is it because he makes me laugh? "Yes."
Is it because he makes me feel loved? "Yes."

It is all of these things, but primarily, I love my dog because he is my dog. Just because of who he is. Do I love him more when he behaves well and love him less when he is naughty? Not at all. My feelings in the moment may change from delight, when he's happily fetching a stick in the backyard, to outrage, when a second later he's excavating a sizable hole in my nice, green lawn. But my love for him never changes. That must comfort him greatly. He is my dog, and simply because of that fact, I love him.

Isn't it comforting to know that this is precisely how God loves us? There is nothing we can do to earn His love; He loves us already. The apostle Paul wrote that, "God proves his love for us in that while we were still sinners Christ died for us." (Romans 5:8, NRSV) In other words, even when we misbehave and do the things we know to be wrong, God never stops loving us. And He demonstrated that love when Jesus died on a cross in our place. There is nothing you can ever do to lose His love; He'll love you anyway. Simply being you is enough.

That being said, there are many ways to grieve God. Disobedience causes God much sorrow because the steps we take along this path lead us away from Him, and away from His best for us. And I believe that neglecting God causes Him to hurt. If you doubt whether this is true, take a minute to read Ezekiel 16 and feel the pain expressed through the written words of the prophet. But even when we stray, and even when we disobey, His love for us never diminishes.

Jesus illustrates this love brilliantly in the story of "The Prodigal Son" (Luke 15:11-32), which should really be called "The Loving Father," since the father's love for his disobedient son is actually the focus of the story. Jesus paints the picture of a father (representing God) running out into the field, in a most undignified manner, to embrace his disobedient son (representing you and me) who had come home to beg his father's forgiveness. The son's choices and behavior greatly grieved his father's heart, but they never caused his father to love him any less.

God's love for you never wavers. It is always there. It is always perfect. It is unconditional. And it is free for you to receive today.

**"For I am convinced that neither death, nor life, nor angels, nor rulers, nor things present, nor things to come, nor powers, nor height, nor depth, nor anything else in all creation, will be able to separate us from the love of God in Christ Jesus our Lord."**
**— Romans 8:38-39 (NRSV)**

- Think about the worst thing your dog has ever done. Yet you still love him, right?




- Can you fathom loving your dog any more than you do now?

- Do you believe that God loves you this much, and more?

- Isn't it comforting to know that God always has and always will love you, no matter what you do? Rest in this truth for a few moments.

*Dear Lord, I love my dog so much. Thank You for bringing us together to share life with each other. I can't imagine loving him more. So when I think about You loving me that way, I am speechless. I can't comprehend it. I don't understand it. I certainly don't feel worthy of it. Yet I know that it's true. You love me with a perfect love. Unconditionally. What can I say? It's simply amazing. I love You too. In Jesus' name. Amen.*

# 15 Out of Control

Usually, when we say that someone is "out of control," we mean it as a bad thing: "Your kids are out of control! Put some reins on them!" "That driver is out of control! He should have his license revoked!" And when our dogs are out of control, it usually has negative connotations as well. An "out of control" dog usually results in chewed-up furniture, holes under the fence in the yard, and pee stains on the carpet. And sometimes even the fear of someone getting bitten. But to have your dog totally under your control—to the point where his will has been completely obliterated—would be devastating. It would essentially strip your dog of his personality, and who would want that?

There are some people who are control freaks, thinking that the world would run better if they could be in charge of everything. It is best to avoid these types of people at all costs. They are not fun to be around. Some wives try to control their husbands to the point of complete and utter emasculation, and then complain that, "he no longer acts like a man." It's no wonder why.

Dogs have wills, and their wills can sometimes get them into trouble. So, as loving "parents," we must teach them that bad behavior has negative consequences. When puppy chews on a slipper, we grab that slipper, slam it hard on the floor, and shout, "Bad slipper!" Puppy doesn't like this. Puppy associates chewing on slipper with anger and loud sounds. Puppy thinks twice next time puppy gets the urge to chew on slipper.

But as we teach and lovingly nurture our dogs, we don't strip away their wills and personalities entirely. After all, it is their quirky personality traits that we fall in love with. Sometimes even the stubbornness and the "talking back" and "arguing" back and forth are the most cherished times together. "Eat your kibble!" The response? "Woo woo," with a sideways shake of the head. Translation: "No! I want sausage!"

If we thought it best to control every aspect of our dog's lives, then we should just get a marionette. But puppets aren't as satisfying to us, are they? Puppets have no free will. They cannot love.

In much the same way, God teaches and even disciplines His children, those whom He loves (Hebrews 12:6), but He does not strip away our free wills. No, God grants us freedom, and calls out to us to choose Him. To choose goodness and light and love. God does not overcome our wills in order for us to love Him. That simply would not be love, and God did a far better job in creating the human race; He did not merely fashion puppets with which to play. Creation was a much grander, much *riskier* endeavor. Some would be lost. But without free will gifted to mankind, there could be no love returned to the One who is love. (1 John 4:8,16)

So in a way, and to put a more positive spin on it, it is good that we are, in a sense, "out of control." Not that God cannot or could not control us if He chose to. He is omnipotent. But He has chosen to decree freedom instead—a divine limitation. And although it is good that our dogs are not "out of control" in the sense that they are snagging food off the countertops and terrorizing the neighborhood, we really wouldn't want them to be so "in control" to the point of being stripped of what makes them unique. Our dogs, and we alike, should use our freedom for good, and revel in the love of our masters/Master.

**"So Christ has truly set us free… But don't use your freedom to satisfy your sinful nature. Instead, use your freedom to serve one another in love."**
**— Galatians 5:1,13 (NLT)**

- When was the last time you witnessed a dog behaving "out of control" in a bad way?

- What about a person?

- Do you know of anyone who is such a control freak that you never want to be close to him or her?

- In what sense is your dog "out of control" in a good way? What makes him unique?

- If God gives us freedom to choose His way or some other way, right or wrong, light or darkness, why do we ever choose the path of disobedience?

- In what ways do you imagine that your uniqueness is pleasing to God?

*Dear Lord, thank You for freedom. In both myself and in my dog. I marvel at his quirks and personality traits, and these are the things which make me love him so much. They bring countless smiles every day that I otherwise would never have had. And that comes about because of his freedom. God, You have graciously allowed me the freedom to make thousands of choices every day. From what to wear to what to eat to what to watch on TV to what career to pursue…it's seemingly endless. You've also given me a personality, for better or for worse, but I hope that the things that make me smile make You smile as well. Thank You, Father, for the freedom to live as Your beloved child. In Jesus' name. Amen.*

# 16 Saying Thanks

Our dog has this odd habit of, after finishing his meal, approaching me and getting right in my face. He will look me in the eye, all the while licking his snout and the area around his mouth, as if to make sure he has ingested every last tidbit of his meal. It's almost as if he's saying, "Thank you for feeding me, Daddy. That was one superb meal!" Is that really what's going on in his big, cute head? To be honest, I have no idea. I'm not sure how much dogs get the concept of appreciation. Maybe they do, maybe not at all. But I like to believe it, so I usually tell him, "You're welcome. I'm glad you enjoyed your meal."

It always feels nice to know that you are appreciated. When you give a gift or perform a service for someone, it is not done with the intention of receiving a "thank you," but it is always nice to know that you made a difference. Have you ever expected a "thank you" from somebody and not gotten one? I'm sure you have. And how does that feel? Perhaps as though you've been used, or taken advantage of, or just plain unappreciated. Saying "thank you" is more than just abiding by a social convention; it is about returning honor to one who has treated you specially.

It is commonly taught that if you are having trouble praying, to follow the A-C-T-S model, where A stands for "adoration," C stands for "confession," T stands for "thanksgiving," and S stands for "supplication." It is not intended to be a rigid formula, but it can be a helpful tool. To be painfully honest, though, when I follow this model, I sometimes find myself pushing through the first three letters out of obligation in order to get to the supplication part, which is really why I'm bowing my head in the first place. Because I want to get something from God. I want Him to provide for me. Now, it may be a very respectable and admirable prayer, such as, "God, please help so-and-so to know that You are present in this time of grief." But still, I often don't linger too long on any of the first three letters. The "thanksgiving" part is especially quick, since I've already gotten through the adoration and confession parts, and the "giving thanks" is all that stands in the way of getting to the part that I really want to pray.

Remember, God is, well...God. Does He really *need* our thanksgiving? Does God *need* anything? In a certain respect, of course not. He is God. He is completely fulfilled. But maybe it's not about what God needs, but more about what God wants. Is He really looking for respect and appreciation? He certainly deserves it. But I think that misses the mark. Let's take a brief look at a passage of Scripture from Luke's Gospel that addresses this point:

> On the way to Jerusalem Jesus was going through the region between Samaria and Galilee. As he entered a village, ten lepers approached him. Keeping their distance, they called out, saying, "Jesus, Master, have mercy on us!" When he saw them, he said to them, "Go and show yourselves to the priests." And as they went, they were made clean. Then one of them, when he saw that he was healed, turned back, praising God with a loud voice. He prostrated himself at Jesus' feet and thanked him. And he was a Samaritan. Then Jesus asked, "Were not ten made clean? But the other nine, where are they? Was none of them found to return and give praise to God except this foreigner?" Then he said to him, "Get up and go on your way; your faith has made you well." (Luke 17:11-19, NRSV)

Hmmm... Jesus heals ten lepers, yet only one returns to give thanks and praise God. (Note that he does so, "with a loud voice.") Jesus' response is rather curious. In fact, it is very *human*: "I healed ten of you, where are your nine friends?" In other words, "You're welcome, but I'm a little hurt and disappointed that the other nine didn't return to say thanks. I mean, I did heal them of leprosy. Changed their lives forever and all..." Why was Jesus perturbed by this? Well, how would you feel?

Note that the healed leper who returns to give thanks to Jesus receives a blessing: "your faith has made you well." The Greek word used at the end of this phrase is "*sozo*," which means, "to save, preserve, heal, and make whole." The same word is used primarily throughout the New Testament to describe salvation. The other lepers received physical healing, but it is interesting to note that Jesus only proclaimed salvation and blessing upon the one who returned to give thanks.

**"Give thanks to the Lord and proclaim his greatness. Let the whole world know what he has done. Sing to him; yes, sing his praises. Tell everyone about his wonderful deeds. Exult in his holy name; rejoice, you who worship the Lord." — Psalm 105:1-3 (NLT)**

- What do you think—does your dog "give thanks" to you for the food, play, and belly rubs that you provide for him?

- Give thanks to God right now for your dog—for his quirky personality traits, for the companionship and love he provides, and for the countless daily smiles that would not have blossomed without him in your life.

- What are some things over the past few days that God has done for you, for which you are thankful?

- More than the past few days, now, but think back over the past several years, or perhaps the journey that your life has taken thus far. Express thanks to God for how He has led you along this path and protected and guided you along the way. Be as specific as you can.

- If giving thanks to God is not a regular part of your prayer life, or not something you regularly think of each day when you receive a blessing from Him, spend the next few days practicing giving thanks to God for each little thing. It will help cultivate a positive and grateful attitude and surely brighten your outlook on life.

*Dear Lord, thank You, thank You, thank You. There's just too much to be thankful for. Everything I have, every relationship, every fond memory, every hope of a new day—these all come from You. It is too much to name them all, so please hear the prayer of my heart. I give thanks. And thank You especially for my dog. My life without him would not be nearly so full. Thank You. In Jesus' name. Amen.*

# 17 Comprehension

Some dogs are very smart. They learn quickly and master complicated tasks. Sometimes you'll see a trainer and his or her dog performing some sort of acrobatic routine on television. It is impressive both in the choreography and in the execution. Soon you forget that one of the performers is actually a dog! Service animals also fascinate me a great deal. I find it hard to fathom how Seeing Eye dogs and other trained service dogs can learn everything that they are taught. Their owners literally put their lives in the hands of these dogs, who faithfully and wonderfully guide them through the maze of life.

Other dogs are…well…I'll say it—some are pretty dumb. I mean, really. Chasing their own tail for how long? Toss them a ball and they just close their eyes, letting it bounce off their face. Barking at their reflection in the mirror. Running full speed into a glass door. Be honest now, into which category does your dog fall? Whether he is a canine genius or just a sweet, dumb pooch, you love him regardless. Besides, the antics of the not-so-bright can provide their owners with hours of entertainment.

No doubt, there is quite the spectrum of intelligence among humans as well. Turn on the television to a science and nature channel and you might find a theoretical physicist discussing the latest ideas about dark matter and string theory. And they are dumbing it down as much as possible so that maybe just a few of the audience members might have a little bit of an idea of what they're discussing. Flip the channel and you'll find the polar opposite—the story of a stupid criminal who unsuccessfully tried carjacking a vehicle. Unsuccessful because after ousting the owner from the car, he realized that he couldn't operate a vehicle with a manual transmission.

It might even seem as though there is an overlap in intelligence between dogs and humans, especially considering how smart some dogs are and some of the dumb things people do. But in truth there really is a large gap. Humans are capable of comprehending things in a way that dogs simply cannot. Dogs can learn how to perform certain tasks, but they cannot master simple mathematics or basic language skills, outside of learning to recognize certain commands. Dogs cannot ponder the meaning of life or wrestle with moral dilemmas. Their comprehension is inherently limited.

But even the best and brightest of the human minds are limited as well. It is amazing how much people can learn and comprehend. I am especially impressed with theatrical performers who have the ability, with much determination, to memorize huge scripts and then perform their roles masterfully in front of large audiences. I once saw an individual recite the entire Gospel of Luke on stage. But no one in their right mind would ever say that the cognitive abilities of a human being could even approach the mind of God.

In the story of Job, the main character cries out to God for an explanation for the seemingly inexplicable suffering he has endured. God doesn't answer him directly—Job is never told about God's divine wager with Satan. Rather, God appeals to the incomprehensible wonders of His creation, asking whether Job is capable of doing any of the mighty acts of God. Job is silenced, and humbly acknowledges that in his complaints he has uttered what he did not understand, "things far too wonderful," about which he did not know. (Job 42:3, NLT)

Perhaps your dog is really smart. I mean really, really smart. At times he even outsmarts you. Maybe more often than you care to admit. But no matter how remarkable your dog's intelligence and level of comprehension appear, they simply do not match that of a healthy, adult human. So too, we must recognize that no matter how intelligent or cognizant we are, our understanding and comprehension of matters are extremely limited in light of God's. He is omniscient, and just as we would like our dogs to obey us because we know that we know better than them, we ought to obey God because we should know that He always knows better than us.

"'My thoughts are nothing like your thoughts,' says the Lord.
'And my ways are far beyond anything you could imagine.
For just as the heavens are higher than the earth,
so my ways are higher than your ways and my thoughts
higher than your thoughts.'" — Isaiah 55:8-9 (NLT)

- On a scale of 1 to 10, how smart is your dog?

- What are some of the things your dog has done which have made you think, "Wow, I can't believe how smart he is!"?

- What are some dumb things your dog has done, or does, which leave you just shaking your head at the stupidity?

- Who is the smartest person you know personally?

- What are some topics that you struggle to comprehend? (*e.g.*, time, relativity, quantum mechanics, how hot dogs are made?)

- If you could ask God to explain one thing to you, what would it be?

*Dear Lord, sometimes I think that my dog is really smart, and I am amazed. Other times I think he can be pretty dumb, but I love him anyway. Likewise, I myself feel smart around certain people, but around others I am in awe at how much more they are able to comprehend than me. But I recognize, God, that You are all-knowing. There is nothing that confounds You. For every question, You know the answer, and in Your presence I am truly in awe. Thank You for reaching down to help me understand You in a way that I can, without being patronizing or condescending. I praise You for who You are, brilliant and wonderful Creator. In Jesus' name. Amen.*

# 18 Naughtiness

All dogs, at times, are naughty. In fact, if they weren't so cute, dogs would probably be extinct by now, or at least all the domesticated ones, since their owners would not have put up with all of their shenanigans. But the cuteness buys them a pass. Yes, it is frustrating to have to replace that chewed-up slipper or remote control, or to scrub the stains out of the carpet, or to have to yell and yell for the little bugger to come inside when he won't listen, but darn it if he just doesn't melt your heart with that adorable face! Still, the naughtiness isn't always instantly forgiven, and a dog knows when he's done something wrong. When he's been naughty and he knows that punishment is coming, what does he do? He tries to hide. Tail between the legs, balled up in a corner. "Don't look at me, Momma, I've been bad." My dog usually finds the tightest place into which he can squeeze himself and dives in head first. This could be behind a chair, in the closet, or even in the bathroom between the toilet bowl and the wall. Getting out is usually a humorous adventure because he's a big guy and needs to back his way out. I usually chime in with, "beep, beep, beep," indicating the sound of a truck backing up.

Of course, this behavior is not unique to dogs. Right there in the opening pages of the Bible we find the man and the woman being naughty by eating from the tree of the knowledge of good and evil. This is the *only* thing that God had told them not to do. What is their response? When they hear God approaching, they hide themselves among the trees. They are ashamed, for they know that they have been disobedient. They don't want to face their sin.

The story repeats itself to this day. A neighbor invites you to a gathering, but you're not really fond of that neighbor so you make up some excuse not to come. A lie. And then, through certain circumstances, your lie is exposed. And you're staring the neighbor straight in the face, and you see the look of hurt and betrayal that your lie has caused them. What do you want to do? Dig a hole in the ground and bury your head in it, so you don't have to face them.

Or there's a certain sin with which you've been struggling, and you have a heartfelt prayer session about it with God, confessing your struggles and asking for strength to overcome. Then you feel really good and determined about being more obedient in the future. But a few measly hours later, temptation comes, and you give in. Bowing your head before God isn't exactly the most comfortable next step to take. You're disappointed in yourself and ashamed. Yes, you will eventually muster up that prayer for forgiveness, but for the time being, all you want to do is hide yourself from God's presence so that His holy light might not shine down to expose your failure.

So we're not that different from our dogs in this respect. When we're naughty, we try to hide because of the shame and guilt. But just as your love for your dog overcomes and you forgive him for his naughty behavior, we know that God loves us infinitely more and that He has already done what was needed to effectuate His forgiveness for our sins. It took place on the cross.

But it's not enough to just forgive your dog time and time again for the same things. You discipline and train him in order to correct that behavior so that he might be more obedient and not have to experience that same feeling of shame again and again. So too it is with God and us. Yes, He forgives us, but He wants us to grow and learn to walk uprightly and not continue to stumble over the same old sins. Remember what Jesus told the adulterous woman after saying that He did not condemn her for her sins? "Go your way, *and from now on do not sin again.*" (John 8:11, NRSV, emphasis added) We must learn from these experiences so that we will not be mired in a shame spiral time and time again. Fix your eyes and heart on God and ask the Holy Spirit to help you truly repent and change your ways.

"Let your eyes look straight ahead; fix your gaze directly before you. Give careful thought to the paths for your feet and be steadfast in all your ways. Do not turn to the right or the left; keep your foot from evil." — **Proverbs 4:25-27 (NIV)**

- What naughty behaviors were common for your dog when he was a puppy?

- Has he learned to behave properly?

- What naughty things does your dog still do?

- What is your dog's reaction when he's been naughty and he knows it?

- With what sins do you continue to struggle?

- What is your response before God after stumbling into sin? How long does it take for you to bow your head to Him in prayer?

*Dear Lord, sometimes I am way more naughty than a puppy or a full-grown dog. I know full well the difference between right and wrong, between good and evil, yet I still choose the wrong, the evil, way more than I want to when I am in the right frame of mind. Help me, Lord, to be more conscious of the allure of sin. I don't want to go through life sinning and then hiding from You in shame. I want to walk uprightly, desiring more to please You than to pleasure myself. Please extend to me Your grace and help me to walk in Your radiant light. In Jesus' name. Amen.*

# 19 Others Just Don't Understand

You understand, because you are reading this book. You understand the intimate relationship between a master and one's dog. There is unspoken communication. There is loyalty. There is love. But it goes even deeper than that. It is a familial connection. Just as an adopted child is no less of a son or daughter to the adoptive parents as is a child born to them, so too is a dog no less a part of the family just because he's not human.

But not everyone understands this. There are poor, unprivileged people out there who have never known the companionship of a true, canine best friend. Sadly, they have gone through life disillusioned, thinking they are just not "dog people." How sad indeed to miss out on one of life's most precious gifts!

It's relatively easy to draw a distinction between these two groups. When I've taken Jedidiah walking downtown on the pedestrian mall of our town, or along Main Street in the town in which I grew up, there are those who cannot resist coming over to us and asking if they can pet him. I never say, "No," and the interaction always brings a smile to all three faces—mine, the stranger's, and Jed's. But there are others who pass by and never seem to take note of the breathtakingly gorgeous Alaskan Malamute in their midst. It's like riding in an elevator with a famous celebrity and never realizing it!

Perhaps I'm overdramatizing it just a tad, but the point is that not everyone gets it—that special bond that exists between a dog and his owner. Of course there is another special bond that not everyone gets, and that is between us and Jesus. Jesus deserves not only our heartfelt adoration and worship, but the most special place in our hearts, for it is He who gives us life eternal. He is the source of our breath and strength and love and all that is good and right and worthy. As Christians, our relationship with our Lord should be the most intimate of all.

But just as people who aren't dog lovers don't understand the human-dog relationship, neither do non-Christians understand the relationship we have with Jesus. And honestly, nor should they. It's not something that can easily be explained to someone who has not yet comprehended the deep and perfect love of God. It would be like trying to explain the taste of chocolate to someone who has never tried it. You cannot fully communicate what it means to be in relationship with God in purely intellectual terms. As much as I love theology, it is incomplete without the experience of relationship.

You cannot actively "convert" someone to be a dog lover. The best you can do is expose them to the greatness of dogdom and let them see how much ecstasy there is in the love of dog, and perhaps that will spur their curiosity. And if not, then, sadly, they are simply going to miss out. And while I do think that every effort should be made to share the incredibly good news of Jesus Christ to those who do not know Him personally or understand what He has done for us, oftentimes the best approach is just to love God vivaciously and let that serve as your "witness" to God's goodness and love. Some people are not going to understand. There is only so much you can do. You can try to explain it. You can live it out. And you should pray for them. Urgently pray. And then give it over to God, who, by His Spirit, works in people's hearts to open them up to receiving His gracious gift of salvation and eternal life.

**"Those who are unspiritual do not receive the gifts of God's Spirit, for they are foolishness to them, and they are unable to understand them because they are spiritually discerned."**
**— 1 Corinthians 2:14 (NRSV)**

- Who are some people with whom you have a close relationship that "get it"—that truly understand how wonderful it is to go through life with a special canine companion?

- Who are the friends and family members who just don't understand the greatness of all things dog?

- Have you had similar experiences in public, when you can easily discern dog lovers from those who just don't appreciate the specialness of a dog?

- Who are those people with whom you are close that know that you are a Christian but clearly don't understand why Jesus is so important to you?

- Will you commit to praying for these individuals as you unashamedly live out your faith before them?

*Dear Lord, I'm tempted to pray the Pharisaical prayer of Luke 18:11, thanking You that I am not like some other poor sap who doesn't appreciate the special gift of having a dog in the family. But instead, I just want to thank You for the gift of my relationship with my dog, and much, much, much more so for the privilege of being invited into a relationship with You, God. I know that there are others who don't understand it, and I can relate because I did not always understand it either until I experienced Your love in a personal way. I pray for those close to me who don't understand. Would You open up their hearts to receive the love You have for them, and help me to model a vibrant, joyous relationship with You so that they might see it and want it for themselves? In Jesus' name. Amen.*

# 20 Sense of Time

There's no doubt that our dogs have a heightened sense of smell. A K-9 officer once explained to me that when there is beef stew cooking on the stove, we humans smell the blend of flavors as one succulent aroma, whereas a dog smells the scent of each ingredient individually. Dogs have much better eyesight in the dark as well. When I wake up in the middle of the night and meander my way through the darkness toward the general direction of the bathroom door, I have to shuffle my feet along the carpet because I can't see what's on the floor. Because what's often on the floor is my dog, just lying there as I stumble my way toward him, not moving. Apparently, he can see me just fine and he assumes that I will step around him; he doesn't perceive my lack of visual perception in the dark. And all too often he is disturbed when this stupid human bumps into him!

Because of the different ways in which humans and dogs perceive their environments, their very views of reality differ. This is true with our sense of time. We are keenly aware of the past, the present, and the future. We know how long certain tasks will take, and we plan ahead. We know to allocate a certain number of hours in a day to certain projects, depending on our schedule. "About an hour and a half to get groceries, two hours to mow the lawn, twenty minutes to shower and change, and that should leave me just enough time to prepare and cook dinner." We think ahead and plan as best as we can. But our dogs do not do this. They live in the present, with no regard to planning ahead. Your dog has no schedule that he follows.

Whereas we have a much greater understanding of time, it is still quite a bit distorted. We live within this time dimension and experience it linearly. A timeline. We're a dot at what we call "the present" and to one side the line stretches to the past, and in the other direction it stretches to the future. And it's constant...or so it seems. Physicists will tell you differently. The speed of light is actually a constant in our universe, and it is time that is measured relative to this. Time starts slowing down as you approach the speed of light. Huh? And that's just the start of it. The more you delve into the study of physics and cosmology, the more you start to realize that the way we perceive time is not as it really is. We see it from our perspective only, but another being, or Being, will see it completely differently. We affirm that God created time and space at what some call the Creation Event and others call the Big Bang. And we believe that God sees time differently than us. If we see it as a one-dimensional line, does He see it as a two-dimensional plane, with all of our potential choices mapped out before us? We can only begin to speculate, but that would take us down a rabbit trail and onto a whole other topic. Suffice it to say, God's view of time is wholly other than ours. He comprehends time as it is; we do so only from our limited perspective.

Back to our dogs. They do not plan or schedule ahead; they are incapable of such higher functions. Instead, knowingly or not, they rely upon us to take care of these things. I provide my dog with appropriate amounts of food at the right times. I make sure that he is up to date with his medication, vaccinations, and veterinary check-ups. I plan ahead for him. He lives in reliance upon me.

So too do we rely upon God, whether knowingly or not. We plan our days and freely make choices, but God, somehow, knows all these things "before" even we do. The quotation marks around the word "before" indicate that this is really not an accurate way of stating this truth. It assumes that God experiences time as we do, which is not the case. Thinking of God in terms of our linear timeline also may lead us toward thinking in terms of determinism—that all of our choices are not freely made, but pre-determined by God. While some theological circles seem to actually affirm that this is the case, I believe that this is a misunderstanding. While we cannot with certainty say precisely how God experiences time—since He is on a higher "dimension" than us and this is truly beyond human comprehension— we do acknowledge that He is "beyond" or "outside of" time in some way in which our best physicists can only help us begin to understand.

Our hope is that when we get to heaven—eternity—perhaps at that "time" we'll understand how this whole time thing works. In the meantime, we know that God understands our limitations, and we are called to simply trust in Him.

> **"I will extol you, my God and King, and bless your name forever and ever. Every day I will bless you, and praise your name forever and ever. Great is the Lord, and greatly to be praised; his greatness is unsearchable."**
> **— Psalm 145:1-3 (NRSV)**

- If your dog were to plan his day, what would his schedule look like?

- To what level of detail do you schedule your days?

- Have you prayerfully formulated a 5-year or 10-year plan for your future?

- How conscious are you of the fact that, though your future is uncertain, God can see time differently and may already know the consequences of your decisions?

- If you sense God's leading, trust in His goodness, and believe in His eternal perspective, what reason is there to experience fear?

*Dear Lord, time is something that I cannot really comprehend. I look back at the past, live in the present, and try to anticipate the future. But somehow, You see it all, and I am unable to understand it. Please help me to be okay with that—to recognize that my limited perspective will always result in uncertainty to me, but that You see it all in some way that my mind cannot comprehend. So I will cling to the goodness of Your character and trust You with my future. In Jesus' name. Amen.*

# 21 Ticks

Lyme is a quaint town in southern Connecticut with approximately 2,400 residents. Its claim to fame is not a prestigious one, however. After several cases of a debilitating disease were detected there in 1975, the town lent its name to the ailment spread by disease-carrying ticks: Lyme Disease. Lyme Disease is prevalent in the United States among both animals and humans, and in the east its primary carrier is the deer tick. Deer ticks are among the smallest of the ticks and can be very difficult to detect on humans, let alone on thick-coated dogs. They are so small that they usually cannot be felt when crawling on one's skin, yet so strong that they cannot be crushed by the fingers. Generally, the best way to dispose of a tick is to either enclose it in tape or to flush it down the toilet.

Most dog owners know the danger of ticks, and many use topical medications or preventative collars on their dogs to repel them. Despite my mother's best efforts when I was a child, our family dog, Dusty, was bitten by several ticks over the course of his lifetime and developed a mild form of Lyme Disease, which caused damage to his hips and other joints in his later years.

Sometimes it is hard to imagine that something as small as a deer tick can have such long-lasting, debilitating effects on an animal. Despite diligent efforts at prevention, it only takes one affected tick to transmit the disease to your pet. In some ways, sin can act very much like a deer tick. Certain sins can be very small and insignificant...or so we think. Yet their effects can be just as long-lasting and debilitating as Lyme Disease, if not much worse.

Consider, for example, the sin of cheating on one's taxes. And I'm not talking about massive fraud or tax evasion. Let's just say that a man knowingly overestimates the value of some items he has donated to a local thrift store. He donates two pairs of pants and a shirt for which the thrift store would likely resell for a total of $20, but he lists the donation value as $30 when he itemizes his deductions. Now let's say he is in a 20% tax bracket. This over-valuing will reduce his taxable income by $10, which equates to $2 less that he'll pay in taxes. The government will never question him and he'll never suffer any legal consequences. But let's also say that this man is teaching his 18-year-old son how to fill out his tax forms. And the son pays close attention and sees what his father has done. Even though this father has always taught his son the value of honesty, the son witnesses his father's deceit. In this scenario, the man has saved a grand total of $2, but he has unintentionally passed on to his son the example of compromising one's principles in order to pocket a few bucks. And it is *this* lesson, more so than the lesson of learning how to complete one's tax forms, to which the son holds on for the rest of his life.

This may seem like a silly example, but do you see how one little sin can have devastating effects? The apostle Paul put it this way: "A little yeast works through the whole batch of dough." (Galatians 5:9, NIV) Perhaps you've seen the debilitating effects of Lyme Disease personally, either in a person or an animal. If so, you know the dangers that a tiny deer tick can bring. So too can a "small sin" have disastrous effects. Take heed. For just as you do your best to prevent your dog from contracting Lyme Disease, so too should you be on guard against the effects of sin and compromise in your life.

"Temptation comes from our own desires, which entice us and drag us away. These desires give birth to sinful actions. And when sin is allowed to grow, it gives birth to death. So don't be misled, my dear brothers and sisters." — James 1:14-16 (NLT)

- Have you known anyone or any animals that have contracted Lyme Disease? What effects did it have?

- What are some example of things that you would consider to be "little sins"?

- Can you imagine scenarios in which these "little sins" can have big consequences?

- What "little sins" have you committed lately? Have you repented of them?

- Think back to some of the biggest problems you've experienced in life. Then trace them back to their root causes. Are there any "little sins" to blame which, at the time, didn't seem like they would carry such long-lasting effects?

*Dear Lord, I know that all sin is serious, and there really isn't anything that You would consider a "little sin." All sin is sin, and an abomination to You. It was to cover my sin that Jesus went to the cross, and I apologize for belittling my sin. Please help me to take sin seriously. In all the choices I make, the big and the small, please help me to honor You. And when I do sin, please help me to not justify or excuse it, but rather to confess and repent. It is my will to honor You in all that I say and all that I do. In Jesus' name. Amen.*

# 22 Hiding Our Emotions

When you live with a dog, he becomes part of your immediate family. And immediate family members share everything. You cannot hide much from someone with whom you live. Even if you are not one of those people who wears their emotions on their sleeve, it is very difficult to cover it up when something is affecting you. Others catch on.

Dogs don't hide their emotions well at all. If nothing else, the tail gives it away. Your dog might not act as if he's all that happy to see you, staying over there on the far side of the room, but you see that tail wagging! Or how about when they're shamed because they know they've done wrong? Head hung low, eyes downcast, and the classic tail-between-the-legs pose. What about when they're excited? When I grab his leash, Jed knows that he is either going for a walk or a ride in the car. Either way, he's ecstatic. I'll be sitting near the front door, trying to lace up my boots, and he'll be spinning in circles, nudging me with his snout, and, as big as he is, trying to scoot along under my legs. "C'mon, Daddy, faster! Let's go!"

Have you ever thought about God as being emotional? He's all-knowing and all-powerful, so why would He have a need to express emotion? Can God be vulnerable, such that He can be overjoyed or saddened? Well, just open up the Bible and you'll find the writers of Scripture attributing all sorts of emotions to our divine Creator. God is the epitome of love, remember, and though love is more than mere emotion, it cannot be separated from it.

Throughout the story of God's redemptive history, emotion seems to overflow from the throne room of God. The prophets faithfully recorded the emotionally laden words of God, where Israel is depicted as an adulterous lover and God as the spurned victim of Israel's adulteries with other gods. Time and time again, He is hurt and devastated as He freely and abundantly pours out His love upon Israel and is repeatedly rejected by a disobedient and obstinate people.

We see it in the New Testament as well. Jesus was bubbling with emotion. There was the heartbreak He felt when He encountered a lame individual in need of healing. Or when He happened upon a widowed woman whose only son had just died: "When the Lord saw her, his heart went out to her." (Luke 7:13, NIV) And there was His outrage at the religious leaders, who were supposed to lead the people to a knowledge of the Lord, but instead only created barriers: "But woe to you, scribes and Pharisees, hypocrites! For you lock people out of the kingdom of heaven. For you do not go in yourselves, and when others are going in, you stop them." (Matthew 23:13, NRSV) And, of course, there is Jesus' anguish in the garden of Gethsemane as He pondered how He would soon, for a time, lose fellowship with the Father as He was to take upon Himself the sins of the world, not to mention the excruciating torture that He was shortly to endure.

So why try to hide our emotions? Should we conceal the overflow of our hearts or let it out? I think that there may be times when it is appropriate to do one or the other. For instance, in the presence of family or close friends, and especially among trusted brothers and sisters in Christ, I think that we should lean more toward being authentic. Paul encouraged the believers in Galatia to, "bear one another's burdens." (Galatians 6:2, NRSV) We usually owe the truth of how we feel to those in whom we trust. But there may be other situations in which unloading our emotions on others, or displaying them in front of others, may be a burden to them, and should probably be reined in. Let's say that you have a minor grievance against a fellow brother or sister in the church. You have made the decision to forgive him or her and overlook the minor offense, yet your feelings haven't yet caught up with your decision to grant forgiveness. In this case, it would do no good, and likely do harm, to express your emotions in the presence of this individual. Or, say, you're frustrated over your favorite sports team losing a big game on a bad call by the umpire or referee. It would not be fair to your spouse for you to carry your frustration and anger to the dinner table, thereby bringing him or her down.

A dog seemingly cannot control his emotions; he is ruled by them. And he certainly cannot hide them. By contrast, Christians are not to be ruled by anything. (1 Corinthians 6:12) We cannot divorce ourselves from our emotions, nor should we. That is how God created us, and as we see in the pages of Scripture, our very God is emotional Himself. Yet just as we are commanded to not become drunk, for it can lead to the loss of our self-control, so too we ought not let our emotions completely rule over us. There is a place for deep sorrow and righteous anger and ecstatic joy, but there are also times when, for the sake of others, we ought to exercise some degree of control and not be overcome by our emotions.

"O give thanks to the Lord, call on his name, make known his deeds among the peoples. Sing to him, sing praises to him, tell of all his wonderful works. Glory in his holy name; let the hearts of those who seek the Lord rejoice."
— 1 Chronicles 16:8-10 (NRSV)

- What does your dog typically do when he is excited? Wag his tail? Run in tight circles? Pee a little?

- What about when he is ashamed? Tuck his tail between his legs? Lower his head? Hide in a corner?

- What is your reaction to the idea of God being emotional? Are you surprised at the wide range of emotions that Jesus displayed?

- When was the last time in which you were overcome by emotion? How did you express it?

- Recall some of the times during the past week in which you withheld showing emotion. Was the show of emotion withheld for the sake of others or because you generally tend to be more reserved? If so, why is that?

*Dear Lord, emotions are hard to control, and hard to understand. Sometimes they well up unexpectedly, and other times I feel them bubbling just under the surface but not breaking through. I don't always know what to do with this, Lord, so I bring it to You. I bring my whole self to You, because I am an emotional being. Help me to know when to express myself and not hold back, but also to know when to suppress a show of my emotions for the sake of others. But before You, Lord, allow my heart—all that is within me—to be completely open and authentic and vulnerable. You will never harm me or shame me, and You want all of me. I thank You that in Your presence I have nothing to fear and that I can lay myself bare before You. I commit to doing just that. In Jesus' name. Amen.*

## 23 Friendship

"Dog is man's best friend." We all know the cliché. Some clichés are, well, cliché. Meaning that they are oft-repeated sayings that may or may not be literally true, and due to their overly repetitious nature, they rarely, if ever, carry any significant meaning. But for a dog lover, this one rings true every time. "Dog is man's best friend." Can I get an "Amen!" from the congregation?

How many friends do you have? The answer will depend upon how you define "friendship." Where is the dividing line between "friend" and "acquaintance"? And for those whom you do call friends, with how many of them do you share your deepest thoughts and feelings? I'm not sure how it is for women, but for some of us men, we've had those guys whom we would consider to have been our friends, maybe even "best buds," since grade school, yet our conversations have never gotten to topics deeper than sports. Sure, there's plenty of laughter and fun times together, and these relationships are truly treasured, but it's just never gotten that deep. And if it were to get deeper…well, that would be pretty awkward.

In church culture, though, certain environments are more conducive to deep conversations. Small group Bible studies, for instance, naturally elicit discussions about beliefs in the nature of God, personal struggles, hopes and dreams, and the sharing of prayers. It's funny how you can get deeper with a brother or sister in Christ that you hardly know just because of the connection you share in having a common faith. If this has not been the case for you, then you're missing out, and I urge you to find a small group of similarly-situated believers and begin to practice being vulnerable. It is a treasure often found only in the local church.

Now, back to the idea of dog being man's best friend. (Keep in mind that I am using the word "man" as gender-neutral. Saying, "Dog is a person's best friend," or, "Dog is humanity's best friend," may be more accurate, but it doesn't quite roll off the tongue as easily.) Friendships with fellow humans, both the deep and the shallow kind, are by nature different than friendship with one's dog. There is, presumably, much more physical contact with the dog than with other people (spouses excluded). I don't rub Johnny's belly and I don't wrestle on the floor with Evan, nor would I want to. It's a different kind of friendship with a dog. It is has unique characteristics and is totally, completely clothed in pure love.

But what about the idea of friendship with God? For some, this is a foreign concept. For others, you've sang songs with these lyrics countless times, and being a "friend of God" has, to you, become cliché. How can one consider God to be one's friend, anyway? Or the other way around. God and people are just so *different*, right? Well, in a sense, yes. Of course. But throughout Scripture we see God exemplifying characteristics of personhood. For instance, He loves the nation of Israel as a father and is hurt when they reject Him. (Isaiah 1:2; 29:13) He speaks to His people through prophets and implores them to return to Him with their hearts, and promises them abundant blessings when they do. (Isaiah 30:18) And when the God of Israel takes upon Himself human flesh in the person of Jesus of Nazareth, He calls His closest disciples, "friends." (John 15:15) Though He was their rabbi and so much more, Jesus explicitly called them His friends.

One of the most difficult tasks in biblical interpretation is taking what was said or written in the First Century (in the case of the New Testament writings) to a particular audience and discovering how to correctly apply it to ourselves in the Twenty-First Century. Certainly, not everything that Jesus said to His First Century disciples applies directly to us. For example, I do not foresee myself being in Judea and having to flee to the mountains upon seeing the desolating sacrilege standing in the holy place. (Matthew 24:15-16) Nor do I feel compelled to step out of a boat and onto the water next to Jesus. (Matthew 14:29) That one was just for Peter. But there are plenty of things that Jesus said to His contemporaries that do apply to us today. Pretty much all of His moral teachings, for instance. And His expressed desire that all of His followers would love one another. And also that we are His friends. Jesus said that His friendship was indicated by the fact that He had made known to the Twelve everything that He had heard from the Father. He then commissioned them to share all of this with the world, making disciples in His name. Doesn't it follow, then, that as disciples of Jesus, we too are His friends? I believe it does. And it is a special kind of friendship. It goes deeper than sports talk, and it is different than friendship with any other person. Like one's friendship with one's dog, it is unique, special, and clothed in perfect love.

**"You are my friends if you do what I command. I no longer call you slaves, because a master doesn't confide in his slaves. Now you are my friends, since I have told you everything the Father told me." — John 15:14-15 (NLT)**

- How would you describe your "friendship" with your dog? In what ways is it like, and it what ways is it unlike, your friendships with fellow human beings?


- How many "surface-level friends" do you have? How many friends do you have with whom deep, personal conversation would be welcomed, and not awkward?

- Are you involved in any type of small group (*i.e.*, "community group," "life group," or "cell group") in your local church? If so, is it a safe place in which to be vulnerable?

- What are your thoughts when you hear the phrase "friend of God"? Does it seem irreverent in any way, or does it capture the intimacy of the relationship?

- Regardless of whether the idea of God being a "friend" is a new concept to you, sit with this thought for a few minutes in silence: "God has called me His friend." What does that stir in your heart?

*Dear Lord, that You call me "friend" is remarkable. You are to me so much more than that. You are my Creator. You are my Father. You are the Author of this universe and life and all that is around me. You are invisible. You are good beyond measure. You are the only One worthy of all glory and honor and praise. And yet, in addition to all of these things, You call me Your friend? Wow. I am taken aback and astonished. If some famous entertainer or sports hero called me up and asked to be my friend, I'd be thrilled and honored beyond words. Yet this offer of friendship comes from You, God, the Creator of every entertainer and sports hero. Wow. Yes, I want to be Your friend. And so much more. Thank You, God, for all that this relationship entails. In Jesus' name. Amen.*

# 24 Complaining

Complaining. My dog does it all the time.

My wife and I will be eating dinner, yet we are evidently very mean because we refuse to feed Jedidiah from the table. "Why won't you feed me the good food? Woo woo woo!"

I take away one of Jed's chew toys in order to sew up yet another puncture wound from his teeth. "Why are you taking away my toy? I want it now! Woo woo woo!"

I have the audacity to sit quietly on the couch and nurse a headache. "Daddy, it's play time and all you're doing is sitting there, ignoring me! Woo woo woo!"

Is your dog this talkative? Does he complain this much? I mean, it's really all about him, right? When you're a dog, the world revolves around you. People are put on this earth to serve you. "Feed me. Pet me. Play with me. Let me out. Let me in. Rub my belly. Now, now, now!"

But does all this complaining really get your dog what he wants? Sure, it's cute sometimes, but most of the time it's annoying. That's why we teach our dogs not to beg. We know what's best for them, and we're not going to deny them that. Yet they want what they want when they want it, and will complain nonstop when they don't get it. Eventually, they may give up and walk away...only to sulk. Tail down, droopy face, sad eyes. "Life is miserable..."

We laugh, but how much are we like that? "God, give me this. God, give me that. I want it now." And what happens when we don't get want we want? I mean, we've asked in faith and in Jesus' name, so we should expect to receive whatever we ask for, right?

Wrong. It just doesn't work that way, and we should actually be glad that it doesn't. We should be thankful that we have a loving Father in heaven who looks out for us, hears our prayers, and gives us His very best. Sometimes this means that His answer is, "No," or, "Not yet." This is where our faith is tested—when what we perceive as something beneficial is withheld from us. Think about it. How badly does your dog want a piece of your chocolate cake? But you know that chocolate is unhealthy for dogs and could cause him a terrible tummy ache, or much worse. Does he understand why you are denying him this good thing? No. Similarly, we may not understand why God is denying us something that we think would be good for us.

And how ought we to respond? Certainly not by complaining. Complaining gets us nowhere. During the exodus, it got the Israelites nowhere…literally. What should have been an eleven-day journey across the Sinai turned into forty years of desert-dwelling. Why? Complaining. After the twelve Israelite spies returned from Canaan, bringing a favorable report about the Promised Land, the biblical author, quoting Moses as he addressed the people, writes, "But you were unwilling to go up. You rebelled against the command of the Lord your God; you *grumbled* in your tents and said, 'It is because the Lord *hates* us that he has brought us out of the land of Egypt, to hand us over to the Amorites to destroy us.'" (Deuteronomy 1:26-27, NRSV, emphasis added) Do you hear the similarities? "The Lord brought us out of Egypt only to be killed by the Amorites. He must hate us!" "Mommy and Daddy won't feed me from the table. They must hate me!" Of course, the Lord had good, prosperous plans for the Israelites, promising them victory over the Amorites and the rest of the Canaanites. And, of course, you have good reason for not feeding your dog from the table.

The Israelites grumbled against God, disbelieving His good intentions and His power to act on their behalf, even after God expressly promised to do so. (Exodus 23:20-33) This doesn't mean, however, that we aren't to come to God in times of distress when we don't understand why things are happening the way they are. God invites us to come to Him especially in these times (Matthew 11:28-30), but we are to do so believing in God's goodness and faithfulness, not with a spirit of contempt.

So the next time that you are tempted to complain to God about an unanswered prayer, take a moment to remember His goodness and His heart toward you, and consider the possibility that an unanswered prayer may really be a loving response from an infinitely caring Father.

**"Many times he delivered them, but they were rebellious in their purposes, and were brought low through their iniquity. Nevertheless he regarded their distress when he heard their cry. For their sake he remembered his covenant, and showed compassion according to the abundance of his steadfast love."**
**— Psalm 106:43-45 (NRSV)**

- What does your dog complain about?

- How does your dog usually express his complaining?

- What is your typical response?

- What unanswered prayers are burdening you most right now?

- What is your attitude toward God in the midst of unanswered prayers?

- Do you believe in God's goodness enough to trust Him through these difficult times?

*Dear Lord, my dog complains a lot. Sometimes it's funny, but sometimes it's not. I know that I have complained and grumbled at one time or another to You, Lord, when things haven't turned out the way that I wanted. Still, I believe that You are God and that You hear my prayers and love me more deeply than I can imagine. Help me to trust in Your goodness through these trying and confusing times. In Jesus' name. Amen.*

## 25 Treats

Is there a dog among us who doesn't love getting a treat? It's a reward for good behavior. It's a tasty little "I love you" snack. Well, tasty to a dog, I suppose. I confess, I've tried a few nibbles myself. Most dog treats are very bland, though there are some beefy chews which are at least somewhat palatable to the human mouth. Anyway, dogs love them, and treats are almost always used in training a dog. You say, "Sit," gently nudge the dog's behind to the ground, and give him a small treat. The dog quickly learns that obedience results in a tasty snack. Dried liver bites seem to be a favorite among dog trainers. That's one dog treat I have not (and have no plans to) sampled myself.

We humans love treats too. Most treats are not nutritious, but in moderation there's not that much harm in the occasional indulgence. Treats need not take the form of edible snacks, though. You can treat yourself to a warm bath. You can treat your spouse to an evening at the movies. A round of golf, since I don't play nearly as often as I once did, is something I now consider to be a real treat.

Overindulgence in such things, at the neglect of one's responsibilities, can be harmful, and even sinful, if taken to an extreme. Especially if we find ourselves being ruled by our desires to the point where these moments of pleasure are all that we are living for. But this is not the focus of today's reading. We're thinking mainly of those fine little treats that make you and your dog smile.

Table scraps are another favorite treat for dogs. I think that if my dog could quote Scripture to me, he would remind me every day of the verse where it is written, "even the dogs eat the crumbs that fall from their masters' table." (Matthew 15:27, NRSV) This, of course, was spoken by a woman to Jesus in the context of Jewish-Canaanite relations, but Jesus did not deny the truth of the statement. If you recall, He actually praised the woman for her great faith!

Think about it for a minute…why do you offer your dog those treats? Why is it that, if there's a little bit of food left on your plate after dinnertime, you let him lick the plate clean before putting it in the dishwasher? Is it really just efficiency—so that you have "pre-rinsed" your plate without making unnecessary use of the garbage disposal? Or is it because you just hate seeing anything go to waste? Well, there may be a little something to that, but I think that when we get right down to it, it's because it makes us happy to see our dogs happy. There's no denying that dogs love leftovers, and there's really no denying that we love to see our dogs enjoy themselves.

Now, we don't even need to speculate as to whether God enjoys giving treats to His children, because Jesus explicitly said so Himself:

> "Is there anyone among you who, if your child asks for bread, will give a stone? Or if the child asks for a fish, will give a snake? If you then, who are evil, know how to give good gifts to your children, how much more will your Father in heaven give good things to those who ask him!" (Matthew 7:9-11, NRSV)

We might translate that to say something like, "If your dog asks for a slice of your orange, would you give him a slice of lemon?" Of course not—you're not so cruel as to play such a mean trick on your dog. And if you enjoy giving treats to your pup, how much more do you think God takes delight in giving you the occasional treat as well!

**"Taste and see that the Lord is good. Oh, the joys of those who take refuge in him! Fear the Lord, you his godly people, for those who fear him will have all they need. Even strong young lions sometimes go hungry, but those who trust in the Lord will lack no good thing." — Psalm 34:8-10 (NLT)**

- What are some of your dog's favorite treats?

- Do you give your dog table scraps? If not, would your decision change if your dog audibly quoted to you Matthew 15:27?

- Describe how you feel when you give your dog one of his favorite treats.

- What are some of your favorite treats? Name a few—both edible and other kinds.

- Have you ever considered that God might delight in providing you with the occasional treat?

- How do you think God feels when you enjoy a treat and thank Him for it?

*Dear Lord, I probably like receiving treats just as much as my dog—I just have too much dignity to beg when I see someone else enjoying something that I really want at that moment. I don't want to be mastered by these desires, of course, but I don't want to incur false guilt at enjoying the occasional simple pleasures in life that You graciously provide. So I thank You for these gifts that I am calling "treats." I love seeing my dog happy when he receives one, so I take it that You must delight in it too when I enjoy a treat that You have provided for me. Thank You. In Jesus' name. Amen.*

## 26 Fence Gates

If you have a fenced-in yard for your dog, there is one rule that must never be broken: Don't leave the gate open. Every time you enter or exit your yard through the gate, you diligently and unquestioningly make sure that it closes behind you, and that the latch catches. If a friend or neighbor stops by, you can't help but tell them to please make sure to shut the gate behind them. Why? Because your dog is always aware. Always looking, always searching for a way to escape. An open gate is an invitation to explore the neighborhood—the Great Unknown—without the shackle of leash or master. There's no question as to this universal rule of dog nature—if you leave open the fence gate, he will escape.

And why is that? Perhaps it is just the desire to explore. To seek out new worlds. To boldly sniff where no dog has sniffed before. Perhaps it reveals a level of mistrust in the master: "Why am I being fenced in? Why won't my master let me out? There's so much to chase and so many places to pee. Why is my master holding out on me?"

Much like the fences that contain our dogs in the yard, God's commands are meant to keep us in line as well, so to speak. But we may have a hard time seeing them that way. When God sets boundaries for our good, we often view them as constraints on our freedom. For instance, God's command that we not take revenge upon those who have done us wrong (Leviticus 19:18; Romans 12:19) is proper in the sense that God is the ultimate judge and that we should also leave room for His mercy. But how tempting it is to want to take justice into our own hands! God also knows how an endless cycle of revenge can lead to destructive outcomes, as each person feels the need to "one up" the other. The "no revenge" command is like a fence to keep us in place.

The opportunity to, say, vandalize the property of one who offended you is like an open fence gate, calling us to leave the safety of the Master's premises.

Now, what happens when your dog does escape through an open fence gate? You glance out the window, scan the yard, and think, "Now where is that stinker?" And then you see the gate, and it's open, and panic sets in. You race out the door, yelling his name as worst-case scenarios flood your mind. You think of your darling companion being struck by a car, or abducted by strangers, or wandering aimlessly miles away, never to find his way home. You search for him diligently, calling out his name, hoping and praying for a glimpse of his familiar face, knowing that he is gleefully ignorant of the dangers that lie beyond the safety of the yard.

The anxiety of searching for a lost animal is an age-old feeling. Jesus Himself referenced it in the familiar parable of the lost sheep. "Which one of you," He asks the Pharisees and scribes, "having a hundred sheep and losing one of them, does not leave the ninety-nine in the wilderness and go after the one that is lost until he finds it?" (Luke 15:4, NRSV) What Jesus clearly implies by way of this rhetorical question is that His listeners would undoubtedly go out in search of their lost animal. Jesus plays upon this typical response to such a situation in order to demonstrate to the religious gurus of the time that God's heart breaks for each soul who has lost his or her way, and that God will search for and pursue such lost souls until they are found, and until He can return them safely to His dwelling place.

When we have chosen to leave the safety of God's dwelling and have ventured forth through an open fence gate, the conviction that the Holy Spirit places upon our hearts serves as the voice of God, calling us home. Of course, it is our choice whether to heed the call or continue to wander in dangerous territory. Much like the relief we ultimately feel when we spot our wandering dog and return him to safety, so too let us grant God that same satisfaction by returning to Him and learning to not exit the safety and comfort of His dwelling again by passing through that same fence gate.

**"Just so, I tell you, there will be more joy in heaven over one sinner who repents than over ninety-nine righteous persons who need no repentance." — Luke 15:7 (NRSV)**

- Can you recall a time when your dog escaped through an open fence gate, or somehow got loose? What thoughts ran through your mind?

- Assuming that the situation got resolved well, on a scale of 1 to 10, how relieved did you feel afterward?

- What are some of God's commands that can cause you to feel "fenced in"?

- Recall the last time that you "left the yard" as it were. What caused you to make that decision? How did you sense God calling after you?

- What open fence gates tempt you now? How will you decide to shut them so that the temptation to exit through them will not overwhelm you?

*Dear Lord, I know the feeling of uneasiness and anxiety when my dog has left the safety of the yard and is in perilous danger. My heart would break in two if something were to happen to him. So I understand how You must feel when one of Your children ventures outside the safety of Your commands in order to explore what lies beyond the fence, being ignorant of the terrible peril that might befall him or her. I admit that I have been there, and I have grieved You. Help me to learn from those past experiences. I want to commune with You, God, in the safety of Your pastures. Help me to recognize those "open gates" for what they are—temptations to disobey Your good commands—and to shut them before the urge to sneak out becomes too great. It is peace with You where I seek to find my rest. In Jesus' name. Amen.*

# 27 Discontentment

One morning, I was lying on the floor next to Jedidiah while he happily chewed on a nylon bone. So I took the tennis ball lying on the floor next to me and started playing with it. Jed, seeing how much fun I was having with the ball, dropped his bone and snatched the tennis ball away from me. "Okay," I thought, "he must really want his tennis ball." So I grabbed his discarded bone and pretended to chew on it. Well, the tennis ball immediately lost its appeal; Jed promptly dropped it and took the bone away from me.

A similar thing happened once while my wife and I were preparing dinner. My wife generously tossed Jedidiah a nice, big cabbage leaf, which he happily accepted and brought into the living room to enjoy. However, smelling the aroma of other meal ingredients wafting out from the kitchen, Jed quickly returned, using his cuteness to try to coax my wife or me into tossing him another treat. Apparently, the prospect of something else falling his way from the kitchen counter was more appealing than the soggy, half-eaten cabbage leaf now lying on the living room carpet.

Never content with what they have, dogs will quickly drop their toys and treats to see what *else* they can get.

Aren't we the same?

We live in an apartment and dream of owning our first home. And once we get it, it is wonderful…for a time. Then we dream of getting a nicer, bigger house, forgetting the upgrade from apartment living that we currently enjoy.

We love our new computer, smart phone, set of golf clubs, or whatever. It is wonderful…until a newer and better model hits the market. Then all we can see are the deficiencies in what we have compared to the better one that we covet.

You've probably heard the famous quote by John D. Rockefeller when he was asked in an interview how much more money he needed to acquire before he would be satisfied. His answer: "One more dollar."

It's the lure of *what else* is out there that hooks us. "I'll just play one more hand of Texas Hold'em, because I'm bound to get that killer hand and take the big pot… Just one more cast before I take the boat in, because I'm sure that monster largemouth is lurking beneath those lily pads… Just one more shot at a penny stock, because the analysts guarantee that its price is going to skyrocket…"

What is the problem with this approach? It promises what it can never deliver—happiness. It says that once you get that thing that you're wanting so badly, then you will be happy. Then you will be content. Then it will all have been worth it. But, as we all know, the truth is that even if the object of your lust falls within your grasp, it does not satisfy. Satisfaction is elusive—it can only be obtained by getting that *next* object of your affection. It is a never-ending cycle which taunts us but never delivers.

Remember the commandment, "You shall not covet"? Yeah, it's one of the Big Ten, and for good reason. God knows that our happiness can only be found in Him. Any attempt to fulfill that longing with something else will never satisfy. The apostle Paul learned this truth and shared it with his readers:

> I have learned to be content with whatever I have. I know what it is to have little, and I know what it is to have plenty. In any and all circumstances I have learned the secret of being well-fed and of going hungry, of having plenty and of being in need. I can do all things through him who strengthens me. (Philippians 4:11-13, NRSV)

Paul had riches and poverty, fame and anonymity, praise and disgust. Yet he learned that amidst the turmoil that was his life, peace and contentment came only in knowing and abiding in the Lord Jesus Christ.

> "Yet true godliness with contentment is itself great wealth. After all, we brought nothing with us when we came into the world, and we can't take anything with us when we leave it."
> — 1 Timothy 6:6-7 (NLT)

- In what circumstances has your dog displayed an attitude of discontentment?

- In what circumstances have you longed for something and gotten it? Did it bring the fulfillment for which you had hoped?

- What is it that you would like right now that you think would make you happy?

- Honestly, how do you think you would feel if it were given to you right now? How long would that feeling last?

- What can you do to learn to be content with only those things you currently possess?

*Dear Lord, there are many things that I long for in my life. Some of these are noble aspirations and others are simply things that I think I would enjoy. Help me to acquire the posture to be content with or without them, God, and simply be satisfied and happy in You. Guard my heart from lust and covetousness, and fill me with Your Spirit. In Jesus' name. Amen.*

# 28 Loved by the Lord

The name "Jedidiah" means "loved by the Lord." Our dog, Jedidiah, knows that He is loved. I'm not quite sure he totally gets the whole God thing, but, at the very least, he knows that he is loved by his parents. He is excited to see us when we return home. We are excited to see him too. When I hear my wife pull in the driveway and I tell him, "Mommy's home!" it doesn't matter how sleepy he is or what he's been doing. He'll jump right up, tail wagging crazily, and run to the window, vocalizing his excitement with a chorus of elongated woo-woos. And then it's down to the front door to spin around and lean into his beloved Mommy as she smiles brightly and gives him hugs and kisses. You'd have thought this was a joyous homecoming after a six-month absence. Nope, it happens nearly every day.

Jed is so happy to see his Mommy, and so at home and comfortable around us, because he knows that he is loved. He doesn't strive to earn our acceptance. He doesn't even think about "what if" things were different. This is the reality he knows. He is loved. There is no other way.

Oh, that we could come to that place before God! To be so assured of His love, to never feel the need to try to please Him, but to just rest in His grace. But all too often we fall into the trap of trying to please God. "Wait a minute," you say, "trying to please God is a bad thing? Don't we want God to be pleased with us?" Yes, of course we do, but the ironic thing is that the more we try to please God—with our actions, devotional times, service, obedience, etc. (which are all good things in and of themselves)—the more we set ourselves up for failure. Because instead of pleasing God, we're actually trying to please our made-up conception of who we imagine God to be. And in so doing, our faulty understanding of God will never be pleased because we will never measure up to the impossible standard we have set for ourselves at which to perform. If your Christian life has been defined as an attempt to please God, then you'll understand what I mean. If you've been striving for obedience, because you think that's what pleases God, how's that been going for you? I predict that it's been full of ups and downs—a rollercoaster ride—in which there are seasons of obedience, during which you experience joy, and times of failure, in which you experience shame. But is it really joy you experience during the highs, or is it just the relief that accompanies a lack of shame?

Thankfully, God is not interested in our efforts to please Him. What He asks of us is simply to trust Him. What does it mean to trust God? This is actually a very difficult and profound question, worthy of long discussion. I'm not so sure that it can be boiled down to a single answer or formula. It encapsulates relationship with God. If someone asks, "How do you love your spouse?" can you really sum it up in a one or two sentence answer? Trusting God means knowing Him, walking with Him, being guided by His Spirit, searching Scripture for its meaning, having a rich prayer life, enabling His love for you to overflow to others, etc. And there's so much more. It's a rich treasure. It's life in the kingdom. It's life abundant. And it's available only through Jesus.

Do you really want to please God? Well, then trust Him. And all that this entails. Don't try to please Him. I predict that if you begin the process of learning to simply trust Him, and growing in a more intimate relationship with Him, you will end up bearing more kingdom fruit than if you focused all your efforts on trying to please Him. And in the cultivation of your relationship with Him, ironically, I believe that God will be far more pleased. And you will experience far less shame. Remember, you too are "Jedidiah." You are the Lord's beloved.

**"I prayed to the Lord, and he answered me. He freed me from all my fears. Those who look to him for help will be radiant with joy; no shadow of shame will darken their faces."**
**— Psalm 34:4-5 (NLT)**

- Do you think that your dog has any doubt about how much you love him?

- How does your dog react when you or your spouse return home after being out all day?

- How would you describe your motivation for honoring God's lordship in your life—are you primarily trying to please God, or is your focus more on trusting God?

- If you have been trying to please God by obedience, service, disciplines, etc., how has that been working for you?

- In your own words, what does it mean to trust God?

*Dear Lord, I've spent far too much time trying to please You, rather than simply trusting You and resting in Your embrace. I've had a hard time simply believing that You love me and that You are pleased with me because I am Your beloved. Please help transform my mind—my very way of viewing myself before You. I know that the only way to live without shame is to walk with You, not striving to please You—because I can't DO anything to make You happy with me. This assumes that You are not happy with me unless I act in order to please You, and I know that this is not a right perception of You, Father. You are all good and loving. Help me to simply embrace these truths. In Jesus' name. Amen.*

# 29 Healing

Thankfully it was only "minor" surgery. Jed had developed a small growth on his eyelid. It didn't seem to bother him at all, and the vet said to just keep an eye on it. But in the course of nine months, it had grown to about six times its original size and occasionally bled. It was time to remove it surgically before it posed too big of a problem.

The surgery went well. The skilled vet was able to remove the growth and stitch the eyelid back together. Because the eyelid is rich in blood vessels, the healing process was fairly quick. But due to the possibility of Jed scratching or pawing at his eye before it fully healed, he was required to wear a protective collar. An e-collar. That giant, cone-shaped piece of plastic around the head that makes dogs look sad and pathetic. I think Jed thought of it more as an "a-collar," with the "a" standing for "annoyance" because it constantly got in his way, always catching the sides of door frames and dressers and making eating and drinking quite a chore. Ascending carpeted stairs probably posed the biggest challenge, as the collar tended to get hung up on each step.

Aside from being an annoyance to Jed, I think he might also have viewed it as a "p-collar"—a collar of punishment. Yes, when I tried to muzzle him the morning of the surgery before bringing him to the vet, he was bad...very bad. And I was mad at him...very mad. After a lot of fighting and yelling and some minor damage to a wall and wooden chair, I finally, and safely, got him muzzled. But I was upset and he knew it. So the next few days, with a pathetic look and big brown eyes, one of which had the fur around it partially shaved because of the surgery, Jed would come up to me, put his head in my lap as best he could with the big, plastic cone, and give me a look that said, "Daddy, I'm sorry. Can you please take the collar off now?" I would try to comfort him and explain to him that he wasn't being punished—that the collar was there for his own protection and that he'd only have to wear it for about ten days—but I don't think the message sank in.

How could I get my dog to understand that the angst and frustration under which he was suffering was not punishment? Yes, he was bad, but I forgave him and moved on. He didn't do anything to deserve the ordeal of surgery and the e-collar; they were necessary and done for his own good. For his health and ultimate goodness and well-being. But from his perspective, that was difficult to see or comprehend.

So as I tried to explain this to him to no avail, I got to thinking, "How many times have I been through some ordeal, not knowing why, or perhaps even feeling as though I deserved it as punishment for some sin, when there was a completely different explanation that had nothing to do with what I had done or failed to do? How often does God look down on me and know that I was simply a victim of circumstance, as Jed was with the eyelid growth, and do what it takes to make me whole again, knowing that I won't be able to understand that the pain and frustration I might experience are necessary for the healing process to take place?"

As it often does, it comes down to an issue of trust. Yes, there is evil and suffering in this world which I believe God detests. But sometimes the pain we must undergo is simply a necessary part of the healing process for the trouble in which we've sometimes innocently found ourselves. During these times, we've got to see through the temporal and trust in God's infinite goodness and in His loving intentions for us. And then lean on Him to help us through the healing process, no matter how long it takes.

"The Lord is my shepherd, I lack nothing. He makes me lie down in green pastures, he leads me beside quiet waters, he refreshes my soul. He guides me along the right paths for his name's sake. Even though I walk through the darkest valley, I will fear no evil, for you are with me; your rod and your staff, they comfort me." — **Psalm 23:1-4 (NIV)**

- Have you ever had to use an e-collar on your dog? How did he deal with it?

- How does your dog usually react when he thinks he is being punished?

- How do you comfort or reassure your dog when he thinks he has done something wrong, but he has misinterpreted the situation?

- When was the last time you went through a painful circumstance and felt as though you were being punished?

- Might there be an alternative explanation for what was really going on?

*Dear Lord, I confess that I oftentimes have difficulty understanding what is really going on. Sometimes I think that things just happen for no reason. Other times I think that You're behind every circumstance with a precise reason for having things occur the way they do. But ultimately I acknowledge that my interpretation of events is very limited and I often struggle to know what is really true. Help me through these times, God, to trust in Your goodness and cling to You. I may not get answers, but I'll have You, and that is far better. In Jesus' name. Amen.*

# 30 Obedience Training

If you've ever gone through the process of seeing a puppy pass through adolescence into adulthood, you'll know all too well what I'm talking about. It's that difficult and frustrating but necessary time of obedience training. When Jedidiah was a puppy, my wife and I signed up for an obedience class that came highly recommended by our vet. There were eight puppies in the class, ranging from about ten weeks to eight months old. The instructor showed us how to teach our pups to obey certain commands and then reward them for good behavior with small pieces of hot dog. "A hot dog for a good dog," I guess, was the idea. The point, of course, is to reward the puppy for good behavior so that he will be more willing to repeat the desired behavior in anticipation of getting another treat. Eventually, you wean the dog off the treats and replace the reward with verbal praise, which the puppy lavishes almost as much.

Obedience does not come naturally to a dog because he is supremely self-willed and his understanding is limited. He wants what he thinks will make him happy in the short-term and does not comprehend the long-term advantages of being obedient to his master. Aren't we a lot like dogs in this respect? As children, the first words we learn from our parents might be "Mama" and "Papa" but the first ones we really master are "Mine!" and "No!" and "I want it!" It takes a lot of time and training to grow out of this stage. I have known far too many adults who never have.

God's "obedience training" for us, his dog-like children, usually does not involve hot dog treats for good behavior, but the goal is the same. Just like our pups, we must learn to trust and obey our Master's commands, even if we do not understand the purpose or immediately see the positive results. When Paul, Silas, and Timothy were traveling and preaching the gospel, Luke records that they, at one time, had been, "forbidden by the Holy Spirit to speak the word in Asia." (Acts 16:6, NRSV) Why? I'm sure they wondered, but we're not told the reason. Luke records that shortly thereafter, "they attempted to go into Bithynia, but the Spirit of Jesus did not allow them." (Acts 16:7, NRSV) Why not? Again, we're not told, and the reader is given no indication as to whether these men were informed of the reason either. Regardless, they trusted God and obeyed the Spirit's leading.

Sometimes we may not understand why we are to trust God and follow a certain pattern of behavior when it seems counterintuitive to what seems to us to make sense, such as giving what we have so that we might end up receiving more. (Mark 4:24) However, we are called to simply believe and trust that God's heart toward us is truly good. Similarly, our dogs cannot fully comprehend all of our actions, but we would like for them to trust that our intentions toward them are genuinely good.

The obedience class that my wife and I attended with Jedidiah ended rather prematurely. Jed was by far the most self-willed, stubborn, disobedient dog in the class, and the instructor quit her job and cancelled the classes about halfway through the training. Jedidiah wasn't the reason for her departure, at least I don't think. However, by continuing to use the principles we learned, Jed has, through God's grace, become a remarkably obedient dog. But his stubbornness during his adolescence did provide me with a better understanding of how frustrating it must be for God when I act as a stubborn, self-willed child before Him. Since I really do want to honor the Master who loves me, I should willingly obey each and every one of His revealed commands and the prompting of the Holy Spirit in my heart.

**"Now, discipline always seems painful rather than pleasant at the time, but later it yields the peaceful fruit of righteousness to those who have been trained by it.'" — Hebrews 12:11 (NRSV)**

- On a scale of 1 to 10, how stubborn was your puppy during his time of obedience training?

- Reflect upon how much your dog has matured with age and training.

- If not for the training, would your dog have naturally become more obedient with age, or would he have been just a larger terror?

- What are some of the lessons God has taught you through "obedience training"?

- What is it that God is trying to teach you now through this process?

*Dear Lord, teaching my pup was, at the time, a difficult, frustrating experience, but I took joy in each instance that he learned to obey a new command. I'm sure that if I were You, I would get so frustrated with people that I would throw my hands up in exasperation. But I thank You that You are, as it is written in the Bible, "longsuffering." You put up with so much from me, yet You never give up on teaching me obedience. I want to learn each lesson You have for me, that You might take joy in my steps of obedience. I want my trust in You to make You smile. In Jesus' name. Amen.*

# 31 The Call of the Wild

I believe that every dog senses it. Feels it. Maybe tries to suppress it, but cannot deny it. The Husky seems to be enamored by it. The Retriever vacillates between following it and ignoring it. The Pomeranian might be oblivious to it. And the wolf lives by it. It's the call of the wild. That deep-down, innate, ancestral spirit that is there within all dogs—calling, wooing them to explore and embrace their natural heritage. That freedom, that "I can't be fenced in" mentality. That need to express oneself. That pure, unadulterated wildness.

It's undeniable. What do we do with dogs to make them acceptable pets? We cause them to be tame. We domesticate them. Friends, what needs to be tamed? What needs to be domesticated? Only that which is, at its core, uncontrollably wild. This is the nature of dog. This too is the nature of man.

Humans have oft been described as spiritual beings with God-shaped holes within that only God's Spirit can fill. A need, a longing for the eternal. Solomon was spot on when he wrote that God has, "set eternity in the human heart." (Ecclesiastes 3:11, NIV) It's a thought that, at first, stirs us deep inside. It answers so many questions as to the mire of discontentment we all experience but never feel quite comfortable enough to talk about. For to do so is to uncover oneself completely. Unmitigated vulnerability. Like exposing an unhealed wound, since removing the protective bandage leaves one open to piercing pain and infection.

The God-shaped hole within us. But after a while, once the metaphor becomes worn out and loses its meaning, it's just another arrow in the quiver of Christian aphorisms. Taking its place along such things as, "new creation in Christ," and, "all things are possible with

God," and, "if God is for me, who can be against me?" Helpful, yes, for a time, until it tends to lose its freshness and wilts like an old head of lettuce.

But therein lies the danger. To acknowledge the truth of the vacuum—the unfulfilled longing—and then to let it sit so long that it acquires a layer of dust. Oh, now and again a book, or a sermon, or a movie stirs it up. The dust starts to stir as that feeling rumbles down deep. But alas, just a tremor. The sermon concludes and the lights go up, signaling that it's time to resume your busy weekend schedule. You finish the book, and file it away into its place alphabetically on your bookshelf. The movie ends, and you ponder it as you fall asleep, but wake up the next morning with that day's tasks on your mind. And the calling—the deep, godly whisper—fades back into the darkness.

Sadly, most people live their entire lives this way. God whispers and calls like a gentle, invisible wind, almost imperceptible if you're not consciously tuned in to it. Impossible to deny but easy to ignore. This is often how God comes to us. Not in the raging storm, not in the flash and crack of lightning and thunder, but in a fragile gossamer. Recall that the Greek word for Spirit ("*pneuma*") is the same as that for breath. Why does God choose to reveal Himself in this manner? So easy to miss, or to dismiss. It's because He wants our all. Our entire heart's devotion. Like a distant lover, He wants us to seek Him. With all of our heart. And that's what it takes. It takes all that is within us to poignantly focus on that whisper, that longing, that desire, that call of the wild, which is nothing short of God's own breath upon our souls.

Sometimes, if only for an instant, your dog will find himself particularly attuned to his wild side. There's a deer just beyond the fence, and something is triggered within your dog's spirit. A radical transformation takes place in an instant. From playful pooch to ravenous hunter. The focus on the prey. The deep-throated growl. The silent, deliberate stalking, ultimately leading to an all-out sprint as his target flees in terror. It is pure and ancestral. If only for a moment, he hears the call of the wild, and responds the only way he knows how. No more being tame and domesticated. This is who he is, who he always was, and who he is meant to be. Wild and free.

Reflect upon that scene. Soak it in. That is what it looks like to respond to the call. Didn't Jesus say something about coming to bring us life, and life to the full? Friends, I don't think we have come close to grasping what He meant as we live our churchy little lives. No, it's about hearing the call of the wild within you. And not ignoring it. Not suppressing it. Not rationalizing it. But responding to it. Opening up to it. *Embracing* it. What does this look like? It is as diverse as there are souls in this world. There is no formula. And there dare not be, because it is all about freedom.

**"So if the Son sets your free, you will be free indeed."**
**— John 8:36 (NRSV)**

- What situations tend to trigger your dog to recapture his untamed, undomesticated nature?

- Describe what you think your dog is feeling in those instances.

- When was the last time that you felt this longing stirred up within you? Was it a movie you were watching, a song you heard, or a moment of quiet reflection?

- Imagine yourself in your dog's fur for a moment. You're walking down a trail in the woods with your master, unleashed. You come around a bend, and immediately ahead of you is an unsuspecting squirrel. Without a moment's hesitation, without a conscious thought, you immediately transform into the deadly hunter you maybe never before realized that you were. As you imagine yourself in this role, what does this stir up within your heart right now?

- Faced head-on with the reality of God's wild call, how will you respond?

*Dear Lord, I hear You calling me. Not audibly, but with a deep sense of longing and hunger that I know I've always felt. I've let the busyness of life suppress it, and I've ignored it, because it takes so much of my emotional strength to even acknowledge it, let alone invite it into the room and address it. But I do that now. I confess that I hear, I feel, Your call. Show me, Lord, what it means to embrace it. What it means to live from it. What it means to be utterly transformed as You breathe Your life into me. I want to be free from everything holding me back, and to live by Your Spirit in every moment. Do what You need to do in me to break me out of this rigid shell of self-inhibition and live totally and completely dependent upon Your breath for life, moment by moment, embracing Your call of the wild. In Jesus' name. Amen.*

## 32 Take a Walk

When you have a dog, taking him for a walk should not be optional. If you live in an urban area, or in the suburbs with a small yard, taking him for a walk is vital. But even if you inhabit farmland with acres and acres for your pooch to roam freely, going on a walk with your dog is still something that should be a regular occurrence in your dog's weekly life.

Why do we take our dogs for walks? Well, for those who live in apartments, it is necessary to allow our dogs to relieve themselves outside, but let's put this aside for the moment. Three *other* reasons why we walk our dogs are (i) so they can get exercise, (ii) so they can be stimulated, and (iii) so that we can spend time with them. Exercise is essential to maintaining a dog's health. Your dog needs to preserve muscle strength and keep those joints limber, and walking is a good way to accomplish this without putting too much stress on the ligaments and tendons. Being stimulated is something else a dog requires. A dog who spends most of his time indoors will get bored very easily. Home, though comfortable, can sometimes feel like a prison. He needs to get outside to experience different sights, sounds, and smells. And, of course, your dog wants to spend time with you. And not just sitting next to you as you watch the game on TV. But time devoted solely to one another. This all happens on a walk.

Just as taking a walk with one's master is both a healthy and enjoyable experience for a dog, so too does taking a walk with God have similar benefits for us. Yes, a walk provides us with low-impact exercise. We know that this is always good. A walk in the morning helps us to limber up and stretch ourselves out a bit. It's not exactly sweat-inducing aerobics or the muscle-strengthening pumping of iron, but every little bit helps.

While a walk provides a dog with much-needed stimulation in what may be some very long, boring days of mostly lying down inside, for us humans I think the exact opposite is true. A walk with God helps to alleviate us from the stimulation that seems to bombard us from every angle nowadays. Televisions, computers, smart phones, and the whole host of electronic devices available at our fingertips can serve to overwhelm us on a daily basis if we let them. We can easily become slaves to technology to the point where we can't sit still because we've grown accustomed to a persistent barrage of information and entertainment constantly coming our way. Do you leave the TV on in the background as you wash the dishes? When was the last time you ate a meal in silence? Taking a walk intentionally frees us from these distractions. Just walk outdoors, reflect upon the beauty of nature, and tell God how marvelously He has created this planet, and how this reflects His beauty. Quiet your mind. Put away all distractions. Simply be with God. He is with you.

And just as your dog longs to spend time with you, when you're honest about it, I'm sure that you want to spend time with God as well. Even a dog who has farmland on which to roam will cherish time walking with his master. Being alone out in the fields is nice, but it's not the same as being by your side. I'm sure that you crave intimacy with God. It's comforting. It's peaceful. Essentially, it's what we were made for. To enjoy His presence. Getting outdoors, alone, only you and your Lord—it's a time of being refreshed. It clears your mind and helps you to see things more from His perspective. Those little irritations like the rude clerk at the grocery store—not so big a deal. The fact that the umpire's missed call cost your team the game yesterday—let it go. Will you be able to accomplish everything on your to-do list today, this week, this year? You know what? It's no longer a heavy burden to bear. All you must do is simply walk with God, do what you can, and give it over to Him, trusting Him with the results. After all, you're not called to accomplish results, but to trust God.

Yes, taking a walk with God can help us get that perspective on life that we miss out on when we're at home or at work, staring at a computer screen or enveloped by some other task which seems monumentally important at the time, but in the scheme of things, really isn't. There's an old hymn called "In the Garden" in which the lyrics tell of the joy of simply walking among the roses with Jesus. There is truth to that hymn. It need not be in a garden *per se*, but taking a walk with God, in nature, can do your soul a world of good.

**"When I thought, 'My foot is slipping,' your steadfast love, O Lord, held me up. When the cares of my heart are many, your consolations cheer my soul." — Psalm 94:18-19 (NRSV)**

- When was the last time you took your dog for a walk?

- Of exercise, stimulation, and time together, which do you think is most beneficial to your dog when you take him for a walk?

- In a few words, express the benefits that you receive when taking your dog for a walk.

- When was the last time you took a walk alone—just you and Jesus?

- Are you able to free your mind, see things more clearly, and commune with God when you are out in nature?

- The next time you find yourself overwhelmed by distractions and in need of time alone with God, will you commit to taking a few minutes to get outside and take a walk with Him?

*Dear Lord, sometimes I get so distracted by life and things to do that I neglect taking my dog for a walk, and I feel so bad about it. But when I do intentionally make time to put on my shoes, grab the leash, and take him on a little hike, I find it to be beneficial in so many ways. I get so much pleasure out of seeing him stimulated by the sights and smells as we traverse the pavement or the dirt. He needs that time, and You know what? So do I. Because as I walk with him, I also walk with You. It enables me time to clear my busy mind and just pray and listen. And commune with You. And I find You there. Every time. You never leave me. Sometimes I just need to separate myself from the busyness, from the distractions, and get outside. May I commit to spending ever more time with You. In Jesus' name. Amen.*

# 33 Behind the Scenes

My dog's keen, uncanny ability of discernment often baffles and perplexes me. Like when I try to give him his medication by stuffing his pill deep into a treat, and somehow he manages to devour the entire treat and leave the pill behind. Or when, on Christmas morning, he finds one of his presents under the tree and grabs it himself and starts opening it. And it's not even one that contains food inside that he can smell. How does he know? I'm sure you have similar stories that you could share in which you've marveled at your dog's intelligence. And probably stories of how dumb your dog can sometimes be, but that's for another time.

But however smart our dogs can seem at times, even though it amazes us, they are still dogs. The have limitations in their powers of perception and comprehension. Dogs cannot learn algebra, and they cannot design houses. They do learn right from wrong and perceive a lot of remarkable things, but it is only on a limited basis. Similarly, we humans can learn and accomplish some amazing things. Astronomers and physicists are unlocking the answers to questions about the universe that men have contemplated for millennia. Biologists and chemists probe for answers on the molecular level to discover how atoms and subatomic particles interact. Humankind's capacity for comprehension is truly astounding, but, like our dog's, it is also limited. For instance, we Christians believe that there is far more to existence than only what we can perceive in the physical realm. There is a spiritual realm that lies beyond our ability to perceive, unless something in the Spirit breaks through to engage us. However, our perception of this realm is extremely limited.

Oftentimes, there is a lot more going on behind the scenes than we otherwise would have imagined. Take, for example, the story of Elisha and his servant in 2 Kings 6:8-23. The Arameans were at war with Israel, yet every time their armies camped in a certain place, Elisha received knowledge of their location via special revelation from God and warned the Israelite king where they were located. Understandably frustrated, the king of the Arameans sought to seize Elisha. When he discovered that Elisha was residing in the city of Dotham, he directed his troops to encircle the entire city at night. Early the next morning, Elisha's servant rose to find the Aramean army surrounding the city. He was panic-stricken and asked Elisha what they should do. Elisha calmly told his servant not to fear, perceiving that, "there are more with us than there are with them." (2 Kings 6:16, NRSV) We read, "Then Elisha prayed: 'O Lord, please open his eyes that he may see.' So the Lord opened the eyes of the servant, and he saw; the mountain was full of horses and chariots of fire all around Elisha." (2 Kings 6:17, NRSV) In other words, the angelic host was truly present all around them. But since they were spiritual beings, their presence could not be perceived by the senses of an ordinary person. Elisha, the prophet of God, could see them, and God granted his request that, for a moment, his servant would be able to see them as well. There is much more that can be gleaned from this passage, but our sole focus here is simply to recognize that sometimes there is a lot going on behind the scenes, if you will, that, without a special revelation from God, we simply cannot comprehend.

There are always going to be times when our dogs cannot comprehend what is going on around them. For instance, at the vet's office, the technician grabs a needle and plunges it into your dog's hindquarters. "Ouch! What is the meaning of this atrocity? Do you have any idea how much that hurts?" Try to explain to your dog that the injection is helping to prevent the onset of a terrible disease, and he's simply not going to understand. Ultimately, though, he doesn't need to understand. He just needs to trust.

There is a similar anecdote about the spiritual realm recorded in the book of Daniel, in which Daniel prayed and mourned for three weeks, seemingly without an answer from God. But then a heavenly messenger came and announced to him that from the first day of his prayers, his words had been heard. Daniel records the words of the angel:

> "But the prince of the kingdom of Persia opposed me twenty-one days. So Michael, one of the chief princes, came to help me, and I left him with the prince of the kingdom of Persia, and have come to help you understand what is to happen to your people at the end of days." (Daniel 10:13-14, NRSV)

What seems so striking about this passage is how matter-of-factly the angel talks about being delayed to come to Daniel to encourage him because he was battling with another angel over in Persia. *What?* Again, so much more could be said about this passage, but the point here is that, in the spiritual realm, there evidently is a lot going on that you and I cannot perceive. Though it would be nice to understand it all, there is probably a great deal of it that is simply beyond our capacity to understand. And, evidently, God is okay with that, because He has not chosen to reveal all of these things to us. It is more important that we simply and humbly trust Him, our heavenly Master, believing that He will work all things together for good for those who love Him. (Romans 8:28)

> **"I was caught up to the third heaven fourteen years ago. Whether I was in my body or out of my body, I don't know—only God knows... I was caught up to paradise and heard things so astounding that they cannot be expressed in words, things no human is allowed to tell."** — 2 Corinthians 12:2,4 (NLT)

- When was the last instance in which your dog's intelligence amazed you?

- What is something you would like to explain to your dog, but which you know he simply could not comprehend?

- Have you ever been made acutely aware of your own limitations regarding comprehension? What was the topic?

- If you could ask God for a special revelation of something in the spiritual realm, what would you ask to know?

*Dear Lord, sometimes I am amazed and even astonished at just how smart my dog can be. You'd think that, as a human, I would always have the advantage in outsmarting him, but that's just not the case. Though I do fully realize that my cognitive potential is much greater than that of my dog, I also realize that my potential to perceive things in the spiritual realm is severely limited. I believe that there is much more going on behind the scenes than that to which I am privy. Angels exist, though I cannot see them. And so much more. While I ask You for greater understanding and perception of these things, Lord, what I pray foremost is that You would graciously enable me to trust in Your goodness and Your divine purposes when things don't seem to make sense from my point of view. I trust that, when I get to heaven, my curiosity will be satisfied. In Jesus' name. Amen.*

# 34 My Muddy Buddy

Due to a drought one summer, the water level on the reservoir which abuts our property had dropped nearly four feet. I have a trail cut through the woods that leads from our house down to the shoreline. From there, I often stand on a large rock which juts out into the water and cast lures, hoping to trick largemouth bass into a thinking that they are baitfish. Jedidiah loves to come down the path with me to the water's edge. It is easily his favorite spot on our property. And when I fish with a topwater lure, Jed usually watches it dance its way across the surface of the water, eagerly expecting the explosion of a bass strike.

There is only about fifteen feet of exposed shoreline from which I can fish; to the right and the left, bushes and trees extend right to the water's edge. But the low water level from the recent drought had exposed a stretch of mud between the foliage and the water. And because it hadn't rained in quite a while, the mud was fairly dry, allowing me to walk gingerly atop it without my boots sinking in too much. Ever wanting to cast just a little farther in order to coax a bass into taking my lure, on this particular day I carefully made my way around the point of shoreline to my right so that I could cast into an area of this cove that I ordinarily cannot access without a boat. Well, as luck would have it—and with my luck, this was pretty much inevitable—I ended up getting my torpedo (a topwater lure) snagged on a stick that was protruding above the surface of the water. Because the underwater portion of the stick was stuck in the mud, it could not be moved. Not being able to yank my lure free, I had three options. Option one was to pull harder until the line eventually snapped. But this particular lure has caught a whole lot of bass over the years, and I wasn't about to lose it like that. Option two was to grab my nearby kayak, paddle out, and remove the lure by hand. But I wasn't exactly dressed for kayaking; I was wearing a fairly new pair of jeans that I didn't want to get completely dirty. Option three was to keep walking along the muddy shoreline to try to pull at the lure from a different angle in order to possibly free it. I opted for option three, which eventually resulted in success, but also muddied up my jeans pretty good.

While trekking my way back along the shore, and trying not to get snagged by the many thorny vines along the way, I noticed that Jed had followed me during my lure-retrieval adventure. However, whereas my boots had enough surface area to keep me from sinking too deeply into the mud, Jed's paws were not so…well, you see where this is going. Four white, furry legs now ended in four very wet, very brown feet. Each one caked completely in mud. "Oh Jed, Mommy's gonna kill us!" Naturally, this all occurred only a few days after giving him his bath.

One good thing about Malamutes is that they clean up remarkably well. Dirt doesn't seem to stick. I got Jed back to the house, tied him up outside, and hit all four paws with the hose. He hated this, of course, but after a few minutes, they were white again. They just needed to be dried with a towel, and they were good as new. And Mommy would never know!

Keep in mind, Jedidiah wasn't doing anything naughty when he got himself all dirty. In fact, he was only following me; he was not to blame. Still, he was filthy and needed to endure a cleaning with the hose, which he hates so much. You and I probably get into similar messes all the time, after which we need some cleaning up. If I had caught a keeper bass that day and filleted it, my hands would have stunk like fish and needed a very thorough washing.

On an emotional level, sometimes we go through a whole lot, either in our own lives or in comforting a friend or family member. It can be completely exhausting and leave us emotionally drained. And, in a sense, we need a little purifying from that. Time to rest and clean up. Time spent in the Father's presence to pray and release the built-up emotional stress. And sometimes these deep, emotional prayers in and of themselves are difficult. But they are necessary for our well-being. Carrying around emotional baggage can be like having mud-caked paws. You need to go through the uncomfortable process of getting cleaned up to get back to being yourself.

Given the choice of getting hosed off or going into the house dirty, Jed probably would have chosen the latter. But the consequences would have been bad. He'd have gotten the carpets filthy and had to endure a very upset mom. (As would I!) Similarly, when we're all caked in emotional gook, we might want to just ignore it. But if we don't take care of it, the stuff is going to get everywhere. It will spread to each and every person with whom we have contact, and that's not fair to them. No, bring that stuff to God in prayer, and He will give you a thorough cleansing that will be good for your soul, and you won't be spreading that mess around for anyone else to deal with.

**"But I keep praying to you, Lord, hoping this time you will show me favor. In your unfailing love, O God, answer my prayer with your sure salvation. Rescue me from the mud; don't let me sink any deeper! Save me from those who hate me, and pull me from these deep waters." — Psalm 69:13-14 (NLT)**

- When was the last occasion in which you had to clean up your dirty dog?

- How does your dog respond to being hosed off, either outdoors or in the bathtub?

- What do you think of the analogy made between mud caked on a dog's paws and emotional turmoil that "muddies up" a person's soul?

- Is stress, fear, guilt, anxiety, or some other emotion feeling like mud on your soul right now?

- An emotional, cleansing prayer can be difficult because it takes you back to places in your mind where you're likely hesitant to venture due to past hurts that you don't want to uncover. But how else can the wounds be healed, or the stress lifted, if you don't honestly and openly bring it to your heavenly Father, so that He might cleanse you through and through?

*Dear Lord, when my dog gets muddy, oh, what a mess! I can't let him in the house like that; I need to get him cleaned up first. And Lord, I know that I have some mud on me, in parts of my soul, and I need cleansing from You there. But I don't look forward to it; in fact, I kind of dread it, because it's tough to lay myself bare and bring up those emotions again. But I know that it's necessary if my soul is going to be cleansed, and deep down, I know that this is ultimately what I want. So I submit to You. I bring You these issues. (Reveal to God what hurts, anxieties, sins, etc. that you know you need to bring before the throne of grace, and ask for cleansing.) In Jesus' name. Amen.*

# 35 Self-Centeredness

"Altruism" is defined as the unselfish regard for, or devotion to, the welfare of others. Dogs, as wonderful as they are, are not altruistic. In fact, one could argue that they are the exact opposite—they are ultimately and completely self-centered. Someone might issue the retort that a dog cares when it offends its master, slinking in shame with its tail between its legs. But in that scenario, the dog is really not so much concerned with how the master feels, but more that upsetting the master has caused the dog to feel shame. And dogs don't like the feeling of shame. "Neither do I, dog, neither do I." But this doesn't change the fact that dogs are primarily self-centered beings.

Think about it. I'll be cooking breakfast and Jedidiah will jump up from his bed when the sound and aroma of pan-fried sausage links hit his ears and nose. "Woo woo woo." Translation: "I want that!" Or when he's lying down on his side on the carpet. I'll lean down to rub him, and what does he immediately do? Rolls over onto his back, legs up in the air, exposing his belly. Why? Because belly rubs surpass every other type of petting. "Rub me here, Daddy!" Or when I'm on the couch watching television. Jed will come up to me with one of his toys in his mouth. It could be Turtle or Domo or Horsey or Alien. It doesn't matter. And as he either drops it on the ottoman or pushes it into my arm, it's not intended as a gift. Not at all. It's an invitation to play. He wants me to either throw it to him so that he can jump up and catch it, or to grab one end and engage in an epic tug-of-war battle. "Play with me, Daddy!" Ultimately, all these things are done for his pleasure.

But that's okay. This is what we expect of dogs. We don't expect them to act selflessly; we expect them to act in their own self-interests. We just train them from an early age so that their behavior is healthy and enjoyable, and not destructive. We utilize their desire for self-satisfaction by providing rewards for what we deem to be "good behavior" in order to cultivate these traits.

But you and me, we're different. Well, actually, we're pretty much the same when it comes to our tendency to act almost completely in our own self-interest. But we're different in that more is expected of us. We demand more of ourselves. If God were not in the picture, I'm not sure how much we would, though. An atheist has no reason to feel this way because he or she has no basis for defining what is moral or immoral. Without a moral Creator in the story, everything is simply amoral. Such persons can only rationalize the conscience as some sort of evolutionary development to enable humans to survive in society and perpetuate the species. Whatever one believes about the development of the conscience, however, Christ-followers should agree that God uses our consciences to draw us to Him. To make us aware of a moral law reflecting the values of our Creator. And to help guide our way of living. Though God's grace is sufficient to cover all of our sins, His revealed desire is that we walk in a morally upright fashion, doing good and avoiding sin and evil.

The essence of sin is, ultimately, self-centeredness. It is a rejection of God in favor of the self. Our consciences, informed by Scripture, direct us to know right from wrong. Rejecting this knowledge in order to choose our own self-centered desires is ultimately you and me saying, "I want that, and I know it's wrong, but my desire to satisfy myself here and now outweighs my desire to do what I know is right." And so we choose to sin. We choose to cuss out that other driver who crossed into our lane, instead of simply acknowledging his wrongfulness and not letting it affect us. Because we'd prefer the fleeting satisfaction of executing some type of revenge, even senseless revenge that never touches directly upon the other person. And so we choose to indulge in satisfying certain carnal desires, knowing that they are wrong and will bring shame later, because they cause the brain to release endorphins now. And so Esau traded his inheritance for some bread and lentil stew. And so Adam and Eve traded their right relationship with God for the knowledge of good and evil.

The more we choose to satisfy our "fleshly desires" and willfully ignore the convictions of the Spirit, the more we sear our consciences, and the easier it is to act in a self-centered, sinful fashion again next time. And on and on it goes, until our consciences become so charred that we don't even hear them anymore, and we have completely given ourselves over to sin. A dog's self-centeredness is excusable, because dogs are innocent as moral beings. They don't know any better. We humans don't have this excuse. Our self-centeredness has dire consequences. It put Jesus on the cross. As we thank God for His merciful provision for sin, let us be obedient to our consciences and not become enslaved to self-centeredness.

**"My dear children, I am writing this to you so that you will not sin. But if anyone does sin, we have an advocate who pleads our case before the Father. He is Jesus Christ, the one who is truly righteous." — 1 John 2:1 (NLT)**

- What are some of the inherently self-centered patterns of behavior that your dog exhibits?



- Can you provide a counter-example—where your dog's actions were not completely motivated by his own perceived desire for well-being?

- Do you think that human beings are capable of altruism?

- What was the last "good act" that you performed which went against your self-interest?

- What positive act can you do this week from which you will not benefit (other than the nice feeling of doing something good)?

*Dear Lord, I admit that I am a self-centered person down to the core. I tend to think of how anything I do will benefit me, even when I'm trying to actually do good. I don't want to beat myself up over it. I'm human, and You and I both know the struggles that go along with that. But when I have to choose between doing something that the fleshly part of me wants, but the Spirit part of me knows is wrong, please give me the strength to obey the Spirit. I know in the long run that this will make me happier anyway. So in the moment of decision, please provide me with the strength to do right. Because I love You, Lord, and I want to honor You and walk closely with You in sweet, sweet untainted communion. In Jesus' name. Amen.*

# 36 Trusting

"Sit!" I command my dog. If he sees a treat in my hand, he willingly obeys, expecting his yummy reward. The words are barely out of my mouth and his fluffy behind obediently graces the floor. But when I give the same command seemingly out of the blue, with no tasty treat within sight or smell, hesitation sets in. "What's going on here?" he thinks. "I'm perfectly content standing, but my master is telling me to sit. What should I do about this?"

The most important reason for training a dog is so that the dog will instinctively obey. Treats work as a good motivation to reward the dog during the early teaching stages of obedience training, but at some point the dog must be weaned off the treats and obey the master's commands simply because the master has commanded it. The point is to instill a sense of absolute trust in the relationship. When I say, "Sit," my dog should immediately sit without questioning my intentions, or wondering what he's going to receive as a reward.

The benefits of this are twofold. One is the dog's safety. If he is off his leash and is close to some situation in which he could get hurt, I need to know that I can call him and he will come to me. The other benefit is simply the dynamic of enjoying a trusting relationship with one another. Good relationships among people, whether familial or friendships, are centered on trust. I want my dog to know that I always have his best interests at heart. Even when it doesn't seem that way, like when I tell him that he cannot eat that piece of chocolate or when I take him to the vet for vaccinations, I want him to trust me and not doubt my unconditional love.

The most difficult time I have with my dog is when I take him to the vet for nail clippings. He hates this more than anything in the world, and even the sedatives I give him in advance don't seem to calm him down enough. Usually, the vet and two or three technicians have to hold him down and endure his struggling, whining, and teeth-baring to get the job done. If he would only trust that this is for the best and stay calm, it would be a stress-free, painless experience.

As is often the case, the words we speak to our dogs are the very words that God is trying to speak to us: "If you would only trust Me and know that My heart for you is only for your very best, everything would be so much easier for you." "Your Father knows best. Trust Me." "I love you and would never do anything to hurt you. What you have to endure is necessary for your own well-being. Just be calm and trust Me." Trust, trust, trust. It's all about trust.

Remember the Garden of Eden story? What was the issue there? Was it that the man and the woman were hungry and needed to eat the fruit to survive? No. Was it, according to Eve, that the serpent tricked her, thus she was not to blame? No. It was, in fact, an issue of trust. A little prodding by the serpent, and the man and the woman doubted God's goodness and love. They thought that God was holding out on them, and that by eating the fruit from the tree of the knowledge of good and evil, their eyes would be open to see what God had hidden from them. But God had given them this one restriction for a reason—to spare them from knowing evil and all of its consequences. The man and the woman, however, doubted God, ate the fruit, and you know the rest of the story. It is the story of all mankind. We do what we think is best in our own eyes, not trusting God's commands, which may seem harsh and even arbitrary at times, but are all given out of His great love and intended for our benefit. Oh, that we would unquestioningly trust His heart for us at all times, for He truly is good.

**"There is a way that seems right to a person, but its end is the way to death... The fear of the Lord is a fountain of life, so that one may avoid the snares of death." — Proverbs 14:12,27 (NRSV)**

- Does your dog obey your commands? If only some, which does he obey and which is he more hesitant to obey?

- Why is it important for your dog to obey your commands?

- What would be different if your dog trusted you completely?

- In what areas of your life do you find yourself disobeying God? Or at least hesitant to obey His commands?

- Do you trust, *really* trust, that God's heart for you is completely good?

- What would it look like to trust God completely in every area of your life?

*Dear Lord, it's silly, I know. You're my Father. You know what's best for me. You see things from beyond time and space and I have such a limited view, yet I still find it so difficult to trust You sometimes. I know that if my dog trusted me completely, his life would be totally stress-free, because I love him completely and want nothing but the best for him. In my head, I know that You love me completely and want nothing but the best for me, yet I still find myself doubting. Please change me, as only You can, so that I might trust You and obey Your every command, knowing that everything You say to do and not to do is spoken out of a pure and perfect love. In Jesus' name. Amen.*

# 37 At Our Worst

You love your dog, right? Of course you do. And that's in spite of all the bad things he's done. Close your eyes for a moment and think of your dog…at his worst. What he has chewed up and destroyed. When he has dug up the yard. When he has soiled the carpet. When he has been stubbornly disobedient. I'm sure you could name a lot more.

Bad behavior for a puppy is usually put up with a lot more tolerably because it is expected. He hasn't learned yet, and it's your job to teach him acceptable from unacceptable behavior. And because it's hard to stay mad at such a cute, puppy face. But the adolescent stage is when it usually gets really bad. That's when they test you to see what they can get away with. When Jedidiah was an adolescent, with awkwardly large ears and paws, he went through what my wife calls his "devil dog" stage. Still sporting those sharp, puppy teeth, he put many a hole in my shirt sleeves. And he would also jump up from behind just to nip one of us on the butt. We lost a wicker basket off the counter, as well as a remote control, to his destructive impulses. Jed also chewed up one wooden gate so badly that I had to reinforce it with metal bars. Even routine trips to the vet were a nightmare. One time the veterinary surgeon from the clinic next door rushed into the room because he heard Jed wailing so loudly that he thought that there was a traumatic emergency happening. "Nope, Doc, that's just Jed complaining about his nail trim."

Yet, despite all of that, I still love Jedidiah with all my heart. Thankfully, he's well beyond his "devil dog" stage, but as an adult he still acts like a stinker all too often. Stubbornness runs strong in Malamutes, as I'm sure it does in many breeds. I suppose that parents would say that raising children is similar, in that children go through rebellious stages when they're young, and the rebellion peaks in the teenage years, testing parents to their breaking point. But a parent never stops loving his or her child, despite the lack of love they sometimes get in return.

It's the same with our heavenly Father. God sees it all, but His love endures. John wrote that, "God is love." (1 John 4:8,16, NRSV) And God has seen us at our worst. He's seen us as children, when we were taught the difference between right and wrong, and knowingly chose the wrong over and over and over. He's seen us throughout our teenage years, when we thought we were smarter than our parents and we were going to prove it by disobeying their rules. He's seen us in early adulthood, when we got our first tastes of freedom and began learning how all of our actions have consequences. And He sees us in adulthood, when we still revert to self-centered thinking all too often and choose to do what we want even when we surely know that these things are not God's best for us.

But God's love endures. We know this because even though God has seen it all—our past, present, and somehow even our future (God is eternal, remember?)—He loves us still. And we know that He loves us because He demonstrated His love for us in the most unimaginable way—He became like us in order to suffer and die on a cross and take upon Himself the just punishment for our sins. We disobeyed, yet He suffered the results. God Himself, in the person of Jesus, suffered for *our* sins by dying in our place. No matter the circumstances in which we find ourselves, we need never doubt God's love, because He has proven it for us once and for all on the cross. He loves you. Because of Calvary, this can never be denied.

Sometimes my wife and I like to joke with Jed about his "devil dog" stage. But it's in the past, and we don't bring it up to continue to condemn him for it. How terrible would that be? And thankfully, God does not continue to hold our sins against us either. Forgiveness is real, and it is complete. It's not forgetting the past; instead, it's choosing to not hold it against the offender. Our sin has been covered. The payment has been paid. It is finished. Reconciliation has come. God has seen us at our worst, yet His love for us endures. Oh, thank God for His great love!

"When we were utterly helpless, Christ came at just the right time and died for us sinners. Now, most people would not be willing to die for an upright person, though someone might perhaps be willing to die for a person who is especially good. But God showed his great love for us by sending Christ to die for us while we were still sinners." — Romans 5:6-8 (NLT)

- Did your dog go through a "devil dog" stage?

- What are some of the naughtiest things your dog has ever done?

- Though you were probably mad at the time, can you say that your love for your dog has ever diminished, despite the naughty behavior?

- This may be hard to think about, but what are some of the worst offenses you have ever committed?

- Ponder for a moment that, at your worst, most shameful times, God has seen it all, yet He still loves you. Can you conceive of a love so great? What would you say in response?

*Dear Lord, I really don't want to think about the worst things I've ever done. I don't think it's fair to remind my dog of his worst acts because I empathize with him—I don't want to be reminded of my most heinous misbehaviors either. But they happened and they are a part of my life. And though I can hide them from people, I cannot hide them from You. But because of the cross, I know that You don't hold these things against me. You don't ask for a reckoning, because You paid the price Yourself. And when You look at me now, You see the righteousness that Your Son imparted to me. And You consider me with love, pure love. Oh, how grateful I am for being Your beloved child! Thank You for forgiveness and not holding these things against me. Truly, Your kindness leads me to repentance, and I live for You, in light of Your most elegant love. In Jesus' name. Amen.*

## 38 Gifts

They say that, "to give is better than to receive." I say that, "it depends on what the 'it' is being given or received." Most people joyfully receive presents. I'm a bit more hesitant about it. Because what if it's a gift that I don't like or want? Then I have to put on a fake smile in order to avoid hurting the feelings of the gift-giver. I'm not good at faking it, however, and I don't really like being less than authentic with other people. So when it's time for me to unwrap a gift in front of someone who has given it to me, I feel stressed. If it is a gift that I genuinely like, I feel more relief than happiness. Maybe you can relate. Maybe not.

Dogs do not relate. Rarely do they not like a gift. Chew toys usually get played with immediately. Tail wagging out of control, and if the chew toy has a squeaker, it's quite a ruckus! And if the gift is edible… "Oh boy, unwrap that tasty treat and let me scarf it down right now!" What happens on the rare occasion that a dog does not want to eat or play with his gift? He doesn't really consider the feelings of the gift-giver, does he? Nah, he just dismisses it and transitions his attention to something else. And if the gift-giver's feelings are hurt? Well, that's just too bad.

With dogs, I do believe that it is always better to give than to receive. I mean, what kind of gift can my dog really give me anyway? (I mean, without help from Mommy.) At our house, we joke that Jed leaves us his "presents" in the yard. Don't get me wrong. I'm glad for that because it means that his digestive system is working properly and I'd rather have those "presents" delivered outdoors anyway. I'll happily scoop up those warm gifts with my trowel and toss them over the fence, into the woods. But giving gifts to my dog—now that's something I love. I love birthdays and Christmas mornings when he gets super excited, like a little kid, and tears apart the wrapping paper to delightedly find what's inside. I love giving him treats that I know he's not really "supposed" to have but, in small servings, won't do him any harm. Like a French Fry tossed to him in the back of the car when we're traveling. Or the little bit of latte left at the bottom of my cup. Jed likes coffee too, but he definitely prefers espresso drinks.

Some people have a hard time accepting gifts because of a profound sense of unworthiness. I've never seen a dog struggle with this.

I think we can all acknowledge that life itself is a gift from God. The air we breathe, the food we eat, the beauty we see, the love of family. All these things are gifts from, as James refers to Him, "the Father of lights." (James 1:17, NRSV) And with God's gifts, I'd rather not debate whether it's better to give or to receive, but simply to acknowledge that it is *always* good to receive gifts from our heavenly Father. We need not be as neurotic as I get when receiving gifts from other people, worrying about whether we will like the gift or offend the gift-giver. God's gifts are always good. That is a direct promise from Jesus! (Matthew 7:11)

Nor should we ever have to struggle with feelings of unworthiness when receiving gifts from God. In a sense, we're all unworthy of God's goodness. That's why it is called *grace*—it is unmerited favor. We don't deserve anything from Him. But God has called us sons and daughters. Jesus has called us friends. There is no reason to distrust the love and goodness of God. So when He provides us with a gift, we need not feel inadequate to receive it, or an obligation to give back a gift of similar value. We ought to just receive it with a thankful heart and bask in the love of God.

"Every generous act of giving, with every perfect gift, is from above, coming down from the Father of lights, with whom there is no variation or shadow due to change." — James 1:17 (NRSV)

- Can you relate to the pressure of having to show appreciation for a gift, regardless of whether it is something you like?

- How does your dog usually receive a gift?

- When was the last time that your dog rejected a gift?

- How do you feel about receiving gifts from God? Do you struggle with a sense of unworthiness or do you freely receive His grace?

*Dear Lord, birthdays and Christmas mornings are a little stressful for me because I struggle with receiving gifts. I don't want to disappoint someone who is just trying to make me happy with a gift that they think I would like. Sometimes I feel unworthy to receive such gifts. But my dog never has these problems. Help me to learn from him when it comes to receiving gifts from You. I know that all gifts I receive from You are good and grace-based. There is nothing I can give You in return, but my trust. And I know that's all You really want from me anyway. Thank You for Your grace. In Jesus' name. Amen.*

## 39 Being Muzzled

What is the first thought that goes through your head when you see a dog in public that is wearing a muzzle? Is it fear for yourself? Is it sympathy for the dog? Is it curiosity? I suppose it really depends upon the circumstances. For instance, if you see a muzzled dog accompanied by a handler wearing a law enforcement uniform, the dog is usually "at work." Some law enforcement canines are trained to use their teeth as weapons. When the command is given to subdue a criminal, the handler removes the muzzle so that the dog can go get the bad guy. But if you spot a civilian accompanying a muzzled dog, the muzzle is probably being used for protection—both for people and for the dog. Perhaps it is necessary to muzzle an otherwise peaceful, loving pet when "Mommy's little munchkin" encounters a stressful situation like traveling, or when a thunderstorm hits, or taking that dreaded trip to the vet's office. In this last instance, the muzzle is used in order to protect the vet and the veterinary technicians from harm, as well as to protect the dog from being labeled as a threat to humans. Such a label could lead to the dog having to be taken away by the authorities. The bottom line is that most dogs hate being muzzled, and the whole experience can be one fraught with stress and discomfort and fear. The dog may not understand why he has to be muzzled, but it is ultimately for his own good.

Are there analogous situations in which, for our own good, we must be "muzzled," in a sense, by God? Are there times or situations in which we pose a threat to others? Sometimes we have been wronged and we desire to take matters into our own hands in order to, as we see it, "level justice." Others, more objectively, might classify it as "getting revenge": "That guy in the Jeep cut me off, threatening my safety. Tell you what, I'm going to give it right back to him, cut him off, and teach him a lesson!" Does this ever work? Does that other driver ever really think to himself, "Oh, so that's what I make others feel like when I drive aggressively. My, oh my! I shall stop behaving in this manner at once! Thank you, kind sir, for showing me the error of my ways!" This has happened…never. No, it elicits a vengeful reaction from the other driver, and the situation can escalate until it gets out of control. Road rage can lead to intentional collisions and hurt innocent bystanders. Years ago, I heard a report in which an irate driver pulled over, opened the tailgate of his vehicle, removed a compound bow from its case, nocked a broadhead arrow, and took aim at the other vehicle's driver.

There are times when our emotions can get the better of us, and we need the protection of a muzzle. Maybe you've never pointed a weapon at another person in rage, but the thought of doing so might be a little tempting. (Are you smiling just a little as you entertain the thought?) All of us have been wronged, and there is always that temptation to "make things right." It is in these times where God muzzles us by using our consciences to prevent us from taking some action that we would surely regret. He may call to mind certain Scriptures to help settle us down and remind us that He is Lord, and that our primary duty is to be obedient to His will. It is an act of divine protection. At the time, we may not like it, and may even try to resist it. But just as a muzzled dog must learn to submit as he realizes that fighting the muzzle gets him nowhere, we too must learn obedience by submitting to God's muzzle in our lives in these times. It is ultimately for our own good, and we must trust that God is indeed a good, good Father who will, at times, restrict our freedoms in order to protect us from getting ourselves into deep, deep trouble.

**"Do not repay anyone evil for evil, but take thought for what is noble in the sight of all. If it is possible, so far as it depends on you, live peaceably with all. Beloved, never avenge yourselves, but leave room for the wrath of God; for it is written, 'Vengeance is mine, I will repay, says the Lord.' No, 'if your enemies are hungry, feed them; if they are thirsty, give them something to drink; for by doing this you will heap burning coals on their heads.' Do not be overcome by evil, but overcome evil with good." — Romans 12:17-21 (NRSV)**

- What are some situations in which your dog can be overcome by his emotions?

- How do you think a veterinary technician feels when a potentially dangerous dog is brought to the office without a muzzle?

- In what situations can you potentially be overcome by your emotions?

- When was the last time that you were tempted to avenge yourself for some perceived wrong done to you? How did you respond?

- Do you trust God to ultimately handle the judgment of others for the wrongs they may have done to you? Do you hope that God punishes them or shows mercy?

- When do you anticipate might be the next time where you find yourself in a situation in which you might be in need of God's muzzling, and what can you do now to prepare yourself?

*Dear Lord, I admit that sometimes I am a bad person who needs a muzzle. There are times when I have let my emotions get the better of me and I regret what I have said or done. There have been other times in which I have wanted to lash out, but You graciously reminded me to settle down and let You be the arbiter in that situation. I thank You for that, and I ask that You would graciously guide me toward a closer walk with You, placing all things in submission to You, not least of these my emotions and how I respond to stressful situations. It is not up to me to avenge myself, but to walk lovingly alongside You, with my eyes fixed upon You at all times. In Jesus' name. Amen.*

# 40 In the Storm

Several years ago, my wife and I found ourselves renting an old horse farm for several months while we were building a house on another parcel of land that we had purchased. There were no horses on the farm while we lived there, just an old house, a barn, and thirty-five acres of property in the rolling hills of central Virginia.

One day, after mowing the grass, I was cleaning my riding mower just outside the doors of the barn, while Jedidiah roamed around outside. Rather rapidly and unexpectedly, heavy raindrops began to fall. I quickly moved the mower into the barn and took shelter as the violent storm overtook us. Rather than make the 150-yard mad dash to the house in the downpour, I elected to remain in the barn and enjoy the sound of the rain rattling down upon the metal roof above, simply soaking in the atmosphere of the summer storm. Jed joined me inside the barn as well, but after a few moments I noticed that he was gone. I poked my head out through the barn doors where the rain was coming down hard as could be, and I spotted him standing by the door to the house, getting drenched and looking pathetic. My wife was at work and there was no one inside to let him in. I called to him to come back to the barn, but he wouldn't budge. Jedidiah wanted to go inside the house, but there was no one there to open the door for him. Finally, I decided that the best way for him to come to me was to disappear inside the barn for a while. Not seeing me when he looked back, maybe he would come over to find me. And he did. After a minute or so I looked back out and there he was, walking slowly with his head down, soaking wet and being pelted by heavy rain, making his way back toward the barn. I called for him again and this time he began to trot his way to the refuge of the barn where his master was hunkered down.

Eventually, he found shelter from the rain, but not after getting completely drenched.

Some dogs love the water and relish getting soaked, but not Jedidiah. Perhaps that's because of his breed. I suppose Alaskan Malamutes are generally not water-loving dogs since the waters in Alaska are usually quite frigid, when they're not frozen solid. So, for Jed, being all wet was not a pleasant experience. All he wanted was to return to a comfortable environment and be himself again. The problem was that he associated the house with comfort, but what he really needed was his Daddy to rub him dry and provide for him the warmth and comfort he so desperately wanted. But Daddy wasn't in the house; Daddy was in the barn.

Sometimes we find ourselves in similar situations. At times, they can be nearly identical. Have you ever been caught outside in a rainstorm, soaking wet with your clothes sticking to you, and all you can think about is getting inside to take a hot shower? (Yes, it's ironic that it's *more* water falling on us that we desire, but water at the temperature and in the location that we choose…) Other times it's just that we have had a bad day, when everything has gone wrong and everyone has gotten under our skin, and all we want to do is retreat to a place of familiar comfort. Alone in our favorite chair, cuddled up under a blanket. Or sitting on the back porch, looking out into the woods. Wherever it is, it's the comfort that we are looking for.

But the truth is that, without God by our side, we cannot truly experience the comfort and rest we so desperately seek and need in those times. There is a peace and comfort in God's presence that defies understanding, and cannot be neatly defined. And sometimes God is not where we expect Him to be. We may retreat from the cold, harsh world to the comfort of our homes, but at times God is calling us to venture out somewhere a little less comfortable so that we might experience His presence in a new and fresh way. It may be that we need to get outside, in nature, so that we are a little more open and vulnerable and able to hear from Him. Perhaps He is calling us to visit a friend or family member, knowing that being alone might not be the best place for us during that time. Or maybe it's even to the barn that He's calling you. Our comfortable environments can sometimes be a little "too comfortable" and we need to step out in order to focus on being by His side.

When Jed was miserable and pathetic and soaking wet, what he needed was to be with his master, so that I could comfort and care for him. So too when we are feeling like this, we need to make our way to God to seek His comfort and presence. We should not automatically retreat to what we think is a place of comfort; we should always be looking to God and going where He calls us.

**"Truly my soul finds rest in God; my salvation comes from him. Truly he is my rock and my salvation; he is my fortress, I will never be shaken." — Psalm 62:1-2 (NIV)**

- In what situations have you seen your dog looking most pathetic?

- When you've witnessed your pathetic pup and called to him to come to you, did he realize that what he needed was your care, or did he stubbornly wallow in self-pity?

- When was the last occasion in which you sought to retreat to a comfortable place and escape the world?

- What did you do in that time? Did you call out to God or curl up within yourself?

- Where can you go to escape your self-defined comfort space in order to seek comfort in God's presence alone?

*Dear Lord, sometimes I am just pathetic. This world can get me down, and I feel like nothing is going my way, and I just want to retreat to my favorite place. I want a cozy chair and a blanket and I just want to curl up and be left alone. And I confess that sometimes I just want quiet and I don't even want to think about spiritual matters. I just want a break from it all. But Lord, I know that there is no true rest and comfort apart from You. Please do not give up on me, but call me to Yourself in these times when You know how desperately I need Your presence. I don't want to be alone and pathetic, I want to be beside my Master, in Your loving care. Thank You for loving me even when I am so unlovable. In Jesus' name. Amen.*

# 41 Joy

We no longer prioritize joy as we did when we were children. As a kid, what occupied your mind? Was it the worries of the day? What was for dinner that night? What outfit you would wear to school tomorrow? How you would maintain the yard or pay the mortgage or when to change the oil in the car? Of course not. Your parents took care of those things. It was occasions for joy that you dwelled upon. Looking forward to Saturday's Little League game. Playing cops and robbers with your friends after school. Visiting Grandma and Grandpa at the lake for the weekend. Those times of carelessness, when it was just about play and joy and celebration.

But as we've grown older, to what extent have we lost this carefree spirit? Maybe it's because, as we grew, echoed in our minds were the thousands of times our mothers and fathers told us to, "Be careful!" Maybe it's because as we graduated from school and got jobs and apartments and houses and cars, life got a lot more complicated, and there was so much to care for. To pay for. To maintain. Some people dream of owning a large estate, driving sports cars, and being famous…but with all that stuff, it becomes a full-time job just to *maintain* everything. And where is the time for joy?

Our dogs are quite different. To be sure, they do grow older and mature from puppies into adulthood. But perhaps "mature" isn't the right word. Or, at least, it means something wholly different to a dog. To humans, being mature means taking responsibility for your choices and actions, and this is something to be genuinely lauded. But it also carries the connotation of becoming more serious—less carefree. Stuffy, even. Trading one's sense of humor for a sense of get-it-togetherness.

When a dog matures, he (hopefully) learns obedience, but not to the point of sacrificing his sense of playfulness and adventure. A fully mature dog still goes wildly crazy at the sight of a squirrel trespassing on his lawn. He still chases a ball or frisbee enthusiastically. He still brings you one of his favorite toys in the hopes of winning a grand tug-of-war battle with his master. He matures in that he learns to obey his master, but retains his joyful spirit.

It has been said that in the spiritual life, the only thing that will produce genuine, lasting joy is obedience. "Obedience?" you ask. "That sounds like a drag." Hang with me for a minute as I explain. It is at the ordinary junctures of life when we are living in obedience to the Master's commands, by being disciplined to do what we know is right and pleasing to God, that a sense of peace and joy pervades our very being. There are appropriate times to celebrate accomplishments and sing praises to God, but a once-a-week worship service is not sufficient to inject enough joy into our lives to get us through the next seven days. Lack of obedience to living in step with our Lord produces something called cognitive dissonance—a contradiction within us—where we know that we are walking out of step and, thus, feel convicted at all times. How can we live with joy when we are disobedient to the One we love? We cannot. That is why obedience leads to joy.

Our dogs demonstrate this well. When they obey us, we are happy, and they, in turn, are happy. When they disobey, we get upset, and then they get upset. Consistent obedience in the little things of life leads to joy throughout our days, and a peace, "which surpasses all understanding." (Philippians 4:7, NRSV)

**"Always be full of joy in the Lord. I say it again—rejoice! ... Then you will experience God's peace, which exceeds anything we can understand. His peace will guard your hearts and minds as you live in Christ Jesus." — Philippians 4:4,7 (NLT)**

- How does your dog model what it means to be carefree?

- What can you learn from your dog about the connection between obedience and joyful living?

- What are some of the things that brought you joy as a child?

- Do you ever sense a contradiction within yourself brought about by disobedience to how you know Jesus would have you live?

- In what areas of your life must you repent and choose to return to obedient living?

- Does the thought of obedience and its resulting joy bring you hope? *(Hint: It should!)*

*Dear Lord, I confess: I want to be a genuinely joyful person! I want this every day of my life—to live with a smile and not with a scowl. But I also know that I cannot force it and I am not willing to fake it. It needs to be genuine, therefore it needs to come from within me, from my heart. But I know that change is required. Instead of living a contradiction, I need to align my choices, my actions, yes, even my thoughts, in obedience to Your revealed will. Help me, Father, I pray. Teach me obedience, and I look forward to the resulting joy that will inevitably follow as I walk in step with You. In Jesus' name. Amen.*

# 42 Getting Worked Up Over the Littlest Things

Dogs sometimes get worked up over the littlest things. They get upset over the most inconsequential inconveniences. Like when a toy rolls somewhere on the floor to a place where it is difficult to retrieve. And sometimes not even that difficult! "Jed, just reach for it with your paw. You can get it!" But no, he shakes his head and woo woos and stares at it. And then he stares at me and woo woos some more: "Daddy, get that for me, will you? What are you waiting for?" Forget the fact that there are eleven other toys lying all around on the floor. The one he was playing with is sort of inconveniently out of reach.

Or what about a dog's sense of territoriality. If another dog just walks by on the street, getting in proximity to his yard, the barking ensues: "You're not allowed around here! Git!!!" Or a wild animal in the yard. Don't get me started on squirrels. I always know when there's a deer nearby—I can tell from the deep resonation of Jed's growl. Heck, I've seen him go absolutely nuts over a turtle walking through the yard. A turtle!

Maybe these things would seem like minor disturbances—if that—to you or me, but apparently they mean a whole lot more to Jedidiah. But then again, it forces me to look in the mirror. How many times do I fly off the handle at something minor? The internet went down momentarily. We're out of eggs. Traffic. During football season, I become way too emotional over the state of my fantasy football team. My quarterback throws an interception and I pound the couch, genuinely upset. Maybe I even let loose some words that I have no business uttering.

We are taught as children to not cry over spilled milk. Meaning, "Child, there's no need to get upset over something so trivial." It is good advice and makes a ton of sense, so why is this a lesson that is so hard to learn? Trivialities appear more than trivial when they occupy our focus. If we allow ourselves to be consumed by the little, they are no longer little in our eyes. If you are consumed by maintaining the perfect lawn, that bare spot or that dandelion patch will aggravate you to no end. So what's the solution? *Perspective.* When someone is grieving over some life tragedy, the petty annoyances are just that—petty annoyances. You don't see someone who just survived a major traffic accident without a scratch complaining that their plastic license plate holder got busted. They are thankful to be alive and to be able to walk away. But if you return from a store to your parked car and find that someone has dented your bumper…oh man, that's tragic!

So how do we gain this perspective without first enduring some grand tragedy? By focusing on the bigger things in life. Ponder God's greatness and goodness. Ask Him to give you a heart for the things that matter most to Him. Pray, pray, pray. All throughout the day. Practice tempering your emotions when the minor annoyances come. Tell yourself, "In light of God, this little thing is just that—a little thing. It need not ruin my day." The alternative is to get grumpier and grumpier and grumpier.

If you struggle with perfectionism and cannot stand any little thing being out of place, try lowering your standards. Think about it—if you feel the need to have every picture in the house perfectly level, how level is level? I mean, really? There is a degree of imperfection in everything. The picture can only be as level as your measuring device allows. Let that register for a second—nothing is perfect, and it never will be. So if you realize that you are satisfied with a 99.5% measure of level, decrease that in your mind to 97%. If that picture is just a hair unlevel, tell yourself, "That's okay." If there are a couple of bare spots in the yard, that's okay. Look at the rest of the yard—how green and lush it is. Create a standard of acceptability in your mind and resolve yourself to be content with that.

We should be learning from our dogs. Sometimes it is the positive attributes that we should strive to emulate, but other times it is their sheer silliness that we should recognize and determine to act differently. Getting worked up over the littlest things falls into this latter category.

> "Since, then, you have been raised with Christ, set your hearts on things above, where Christ is, seated at the right hand of God. Set your minds on things above, not on earthly things. For you died, and your life is now hidden with Christ in God."— Colossians 3:1-3 (NIV)

- What are some of the "little things" that drive your dog nuts?

- What are some of the petty annoyances that get under your skin?

- Why do you think it is that these things in particular get you more annoyed than other things?

- Recall a time in your life when you were in the midst of something heavy. How did that change your perspective of the little things?

- What can you do today to start practicing a changed perspective?

*Dear Lord, I laugh at my dog when he gets irked over something minor, but in all seriousness, I'm not all that different. I get irked and ticked off way too easily over the most minor things, and it usually happens when my focus has been on myself. Help me, Lord, to take my focus off of little old me and see You in the eyes of my Spirit. Be on my mind and in my heart at all times, please. Rescue me from myself! I want to love the things that You love, and be heartbroken over the things that break Your heart, and care more about what You care for. May I be caught up in these loftier things so that the little things won't affect me so much. For Your glory. And for my sanity. In Jesus' name. Amen.*

# 43 Saying No

Have you ever had to tell your dog, "No!"? Of course you have. Maybe a better question is, "How many times today have you had to tell your dog, 'No!'"? Sometimes it is because he is chewing something on which he ought not chew. Or he's licking a sore spot on his skin that won't heal unless it is left alone. Or he's scared or upset and is showing you his teeth with a snarl. Or he's just being disobedient in any number of other ways. The point is that whatever he's doing, he needs to stop it. And he needs to stop it now.

It's so clear to you and me when this occurs. He's doing something harmful. We think, "Dummy, you know that what you're doing is only going to hurt you." So mercifully, and perhaps with a bit of frustration, we chirp, "No!" Not, "You know, Sweet Muffin, that behavior, though satisfying in the now, will lead to regret tomorrow." No, we just shout, "No!" "Stop it!" "Bad dog!" It requires a jolting response.

I wonder how our lives would change if every wall inside of our homes were mirrored. Perhaps we'd see ourselves a little more clearly. There are so many things that we do wrong, and it should be obvious to the casual onlooker. That extra cookie out of the pantry when we should be dieting. That purchase of the pair of pants we don't need but just want so badly. Even if they're wildly overpriced, at least it comes with free shipping! Oh, that internet one-click ordering can make it seem so painless. And we won't see the price we paid until the credit card statement comes at the end of the monthly cycle, and even then we just pay the total and not review how much we've spent on each item. And speaking of one-click ordering on the internet, how easy it is to just "take a peak" of that picture on that website that we absolutely know we shouldn't be looking at? But hey, that's why browser history is so easy to clear, right? Just another click of the button and the evidence is gone.

Perhaps with that mirrored house, we would see what we're doing more clearly. And maybe even have the boldness to shout, "No!" to ourselves. Not a wimpy, "You know that's not good for you," or, "You are going to regret that later." But a sharp, loud, jolting, "No!" Maybe slap your hand. Slap yourself on the cheek. Something to jolt you into seeing things more clearly. It sounds shocking, but that's the point. Sometimes when we're slowing sinking into sin, we need to be shocked out of it. Like a splash of cold water on the face. "Wake up! This ain't right! No!"

If we care enough about our dogs' well-being to shout at them in order to immediately prevent bad behavior from continuing, shouldn't we care enough about ourselves to do the same?

**"Well then, should we keep on sinning so that God can show us more and more of his wonderful grace? Of course not! Since we have died to sin, how can we continue to live in it?"**
**— Romans 6:1-2 (NLT)**

- When is the last time you said, "No!" to your dog? What was he doing wrong, and what harm would have occurred if you had not intervened?




- How does your dog typically react when you tell him, "No!"?

- What is something you've done lately that you regret?

- If you had found the sense to tell yourself, "No!" at the time, how differently would things have played out?

- Will you commit to an experiment? The next time you find yourself about to knowingly partake in behavior that you know is wrong, audibly shout out, "No!" and see if you are able to alter your behavior.

*Dear Lord, there is so much that I regret. I confess that I am a sinner and I have willingly and consciously chosen to do what I know is wrong. Even this past week I have [confess your sins to God]. I thank You for the promise of forgiveness through Jesus, but I don't want to presume upon Your grace. I want to alter my behavior and walk uprightly in the manner in which You and I both desire. Please help me to say, "No!" to sin and wake up to the reality of what I am doing in the face of temptation. Please guide me by Your Holy Spirit. In Jesus' name. Amen.*

# 44 Learning to Heel

To "heel" means to walk directly beside another. In other words, successfully teaching your dog to heel means that he will walk alongside you, not pulling you forward or side-to-side. When a dog heels properly, he will stop when you stop, and go when and where you go. It makes for a much more enjoyable walk for master and dog alike. Master gets to walk along, leash gently in hand, without dislocating his or her shoulder, and dog doesn't feel the uncomfortable jerk of being tugged at by his collar or harness.

Of course, to heel doesn't necessarily mean to march like a soldier, eyes focused straight ahead with rigid, robot-like body movements. It allows for the dog, at a relaxed pace, to take in his surroundings. The sights—people, cars, other dogs—and sounds—birds chirping, people talking, an airplane overhead—and smells—blooming flowers, honeysuckle, animal urine. It is an experience where the master is in charge and the dog obediently and joyfully joins in.

But it takes time, patience, and training for a dog to learn to heel. Trainers use different methods. Some focus on punishing unwanted behavior in order to teach the dog what not to do. Others use the lure-and-reward method in order to encourage desirable behavior. Whatever the method, the point is to teach the dog that when walking on a leash, he is not in charge. He can and should learn to trust the master and, in time, will find that the master's way is best for the both of them.

Our learning to walk with God, in spirit, is much like a dog learning to heel. When we march on ahead, God might, in a sense, give us a little tug on the reins as if to say, "Wait. Not yet, but in My timing." When we veer off to the left or the right, off the straight-and-narrow path of righteous living, God pulls us back alongside Him, where we ought to be. And just as dogs get easily distracted by alluring smells on a walk, so too are we prone to being distracted by the cares of the world. So just as we tug on a dog's leash to keep him in track, God also gives us a gentle tug, as if to say, "Leave it alone and come with Me."

Sometimes these tugs take the form of a check in our spirit—an unsettled feeling that some decision we are about to make is not right. Or they come as the voice of our conscience telling us, "Whoa, there! Hold up a bit." Other times we can be reading Scripture and a certain verse seems to leap off the page, speaking directly to us. For instance, say that you are serving selflessly at church but you're feeling tired and unappreciated and thinking about stepping down from your volunteer position. Then, while reading your Bible, you come across the verse where Paul writes, "Let us not become weary in doing good, for at the proper time we will reap a harvest if we do not give up." (Galatians 6:9, NIV) And you sense that it is an encouragement from God to keep at it. A reminder that you are doing good for His sake. And it reenergizes you to continue serving, but with a renewed sense of joy and purpose.

As we learn to heel at the Master's side while traversing this journey of life, we get to enjoy the sights, sounds, and smells along the way, just as our dogs do on a walk. A dog's nose might lead him to sniff out another animal's droppings. Yuck! And, if left unchecked, who knows where our noses will lead us? But if we trust God to lead us where He would like for us to go together, the journey, no matter where it takes us, is sure to carry much more fulfillment and adventure than if we were to do it alone.

**"Jesus spoke to the people once more and said, 'I am the light of the world. If you follow me, you won't have to walk in darkness, because you will have the light that leads to life.'"**
**— John 8:12 (NLT)**

- How well does your dog heel when you take him on a walk?

- Even the most obedient dogs get distracted from time to time on a walk. What is it that your dog finds most alluring and distracting?

- If your dog were to lead the walk, where would he take you?

- If you were to walk through the journey of life without God, where would you end up?

- When was the last time in which you sensed God giving you a little "tug" in one direction or another?

- Does the thought of allowing God to completely take the reins on your life frighten you, or does it give you hope and comfort?

*Dear Lord, I think that if I were a dog, learning to heel would be one of the toughest lessons I'd have to learn. I usually think that I know best, so I'd want to go where I want to go. Having someone else tell me where I should walk would seem like a hindrance to my spirit of exploration. But as a human, I know that, on my own, I will get myself into all sorts of trouble. To trust and believe that You are in control, and that I need only walk alongside You, takes a huge weight off my shoulders. As You lead, I will be safe and secure. And where You lead me, though it be a mystery to me, I'm sure that it will be more wonderful of an adventure than I ever could have planned on my own. In Jesus' name. Amen.*

# 45 Plastic Packaging

How many times has this occurred in your home? Your dog is lying down, dead to the world. You go over and pet him, and he's good with that, but he doesn't get up. Then you head over to the door and open it up to let him out. You call his name. No response. You call him again. Nothing. So you let him be. You shut the door and head to the kitchen and grab something to eat from the pantry. It may be potato chips or crackers or some other snack, but it's wrapped in plastic packaging. And as you handle it, it makes that familiar crinkling sound, which you think nothing of. What next? You guessed it. Your dog is magically by your side, ears up, eyes wide open. "What treat have you got for me?" The simple rattling of plastic has drawn your dog out of a comatose state into being an alert, focused, energetic dog again. Ahh, the magic of polyethylene with a thin aluminum coating.

When Jedidiah does this—which is fairly often—I usually roll my eyes, but it never really upsets me. I know that he loves me, but oftentimes he's simply more motivated by what he can get *from* me, rather than by just being *with* me. And he's cute about it, so it's hard to get mad at that. And usually he ends up getting a treat out of it. It's not always a morsel of the same thing that I was preparing to eat, but he'll get something because I want to please him. Baby carrots are his favorite snacks. He'll chew them while he stands there, looking at me, and I'll count the bites. He averages somewhere around forty-five chews per baby carrot, and probably drops about four ounces of drool on the floor in the process. What a difference from when he was a puppy and he would inhale baby carrots whole! They would then come out his other end the same way, but now I'm getting way off track…

I think that there is somewhat of an analogy between a dog's snack-motivated behavior and our attitude toward God. I mean, we usually don't hesitate to go to Him to get something we want. I'm not referring only to fulfilling our appetites. We go to Him with our sincere, heartfelt, selfless prayer requests. We go to God right away because we know that He alone can answer them, and no one else. But what about the other times when we could be praying, or just meditating on His goodness and love, basking in His presence? But much like our comatose dogs, we are also physically tired. I know that our bodies certainly need rest. And in today's go-go-go world, we often neglect this basic need in order to accomplish all the chores that must get done. But how about going to God more often when we're not even looking to receive anything from Him? Just because we sense in our hearts that He is calling us to spend time with Him.

Now imagine if, for instance, your dog *only* came to you when he wanted a treat? And when you went to go and give him a petting, he got up and left the room? That would hurt, wouldn't it? You'd begin to question whether your dog really loved you, or whether he just saw you as a provider of sustenance and nothing else. There are beings that act like that. They're called cats. (In all fairness, there are a few friendly felines out there who are not so aloof.) But seriously, though, would you call that dog your "companion"?

So imagine how God must feel if we see Him not as a loving Father, but merely as a divine vending machine that we approach only when we want to get something out of Him: "Here's a prayer that I'll drop in the slot, and I'll press button E3 for a blessing, please. See You next time."

It's always good to come running to our heavenly Father when we want something from Him. I don't think He's ever turned off by that. But He deserves so much more. His very character is love and He doesn't want to hoard His love; He wants to share it with us. In fact, if we really want blessings from Him, we'll get more than we can think to ask for if we simply spend more time in His presence. I believe that He blesses most the ones He knows best, or the ones that know Him best. And the ones that know Him best are the ones who spend the most time with Him.

"And when you pray, do not be like the hypocrites, for they love to pray standing in the synagogues and on the street corners to be seen by others. Truly I tell you, they have received their reward in full. But when you pray, go into your room, close the door and pray to your Father, who is unseen. Then your Father, who sees what is done in secret, will reward you."
— Matthew 6:5-6 (NIV)

- How does your dog usually react when you get some plastic-wrapped treat from the pantry?

- How does it make you feel when your dog ignores you one minute, but then gives you his full attention only when he senses the potential to receive a treat?

- Have you experienced tiredness or laziness as a competitor to intentionally spending time in God's presence?

- How do you think God feels when we come to Him with only our list of prayer requests, instead of simply coming to commune with Him?

- Would you consider setting aside ten minutes each day this week to simply sit in silence before God, listening and praying, but not specifically asking for anything?

*Dear Lord, how You must roll Your eyes when I give You my full attention when I'm seeking something from You, but acting too tired or distracted to give You more of my time when I otherwise could, but choose not to. Thank You that You never turn me away when I do come to You, and please, by the power of Your Sprit, graciously grant me energy and discipline to spend more time in Your presence. It's something I've never regretted. In Jesus' name. Amen.*

# 46 Pride

Sometimes my wife and I will set up a doggy date with another couple. It is a chance for the four of us humans to gather together and be social while we watch to see how our dogs interact. Usually, the dogs get along just fine; sometimes they do not. I recall very clearly one of these dates in which the other dog, though significantly smaller than our Alaskan Malamute, was the aggressor of some very rough play. Jedidiah's reaction, however, really caused me to think. You see, although Jed, being the larger dog, could easily have knocked the other dog around to put him in his place, he chose not to act that way. Instead, Jed just kind of endured the other dog's taunts. He did not let himself be vulnerable or submissive; rather, he just backed up and turned away when the other dog came at him.

I couldn't help but think of how I would have reacted if I were Jedidiah in that situation. Most likely, I would have taken the aggressive behavior by the other dog as a personal attack on my manhood. "Who are you, little one, to think you can lunge at me and take me on? You wanna fight? I'll fight, and you're going down!" You see, I would have interpreted the taunts and rough play as attacks on my pride and I likely would have gotten physical in response, rather than endure the taunting, lose face, and suffer shame. Perhaps someone wired differently would have cowered in a corner, feeling smaller than a Chihuahua puppy, and would have taken the other dog's taunts as fatal blows to an already battered ego.

But Jed, in avoiding the conflict, suffered no shame. And ironically, his reaction actually made me proud of him. Apparently, he wasn't worried about losing face or not standing his ground. He must have known already that he didn't have to prove himself to the other dog to display his superiority. Oftentimes, in the midst of a taunt, the weak retaliate, but the truly strong do not, because they know who they are. The words, insults, or physical provocations of others cannot shake the foundation of a rock-solid sense of self.

Jesus had insults, accusations, and much worse hurled at Him constantly during His ministry. His own people tried to stone Him as He taught them about God. (John 10:31) The religious leaders brought forth witnesses to testify falsely against Him at His trial. (Matthew 26:59-60) He was beaten and mocked by Roman soldiers after being sentenced to death. (Matthew 26:67-68) And He was even mocked while He hung there, dying for the sins of the world. (Matthew 27:39-43) Yet Jesus never retaliated. He never defended Himself. He knew who He was. He was tougher than the nails that held Him on that cross.

Jedidiah knew that he was a big boy, well loved by his parents, and he felt no need to defend himself against some smaller, insecure dog trying to prove itself. Jesus knew that He was the Son of God, well loved by the Father, and did not need to defend Himself against smaller men who were jealous of His charisma and influence. Likewise, you and I should place our confidence in the fact that we are well loved children of God, and that our security is wrapped up in being His beloved. We need not let our pride cause us to retaliate or defend ourselves against the taunts of others—we can be stronger than that. Christ lives in us, and as we abide in Him, we can stand firm against all things that come against us.

**"But you belong to God, my dear children. You have already won a victory over those people, because the Spirit who lives in you is greater than the spirit who lives in the world."**
**— 1 John 4:4 (NLT)**

- How does your dog generally react in the presence of a more aggressive dog?




- How do you react when you feel as though someone has insulted your pride?




- How would you distinguish between the "destructive" pride that involves your ego and the "good" pride you might feel when, say, your dog behaves well?




- What can we learn from the example of Jesus when He faced insults and mockery?

- When was the last time you felt that your pride was attacked? How did you respond? How should you have responded?

*Dear Lord, this pride thing gets me all the time. Very often I find myself in situations where I feel belittled and even worthless. Sometimes I try to speak up or do something to show my worth, but it usually leads to me feeling worse. Other times I believe the lies spoken about me, and feel insignificantly small. Please help me to understand who I am in You. Help me to grow in that knowledge so that I can be confident that I am Your beloved child and that I need not prove my strength to others. Help me to walk upright and confidently, knowing that You live inside of me. In Jesus' name. Amen.*

# 47 Waiting

Waiting is never any fun. There may be excitement, however, in anticipation. The big game is about to start. The concert is tonight. We leave for vacation on Saturday. But the joy associated with anticipation is not in the waiting itself; it is because you know that the waiting will soon be over.

You and I are used to always having a calendar and a clock close at hand and knowing precisely what time it is. So when we are waiting for something, we can count down the days, hours, and minutes. In short, we can tell time. When we leave the house, we usually have a general idea of when we will return. Walking out to get the mail only takes a minute or two. A trip to the grocery store might equate to a one-hour absence. But when the excursion involves running multiple errands, or a trip to a neighboring town, it could be dark outside by the time we get home. And what do our dogs think about this? "Daddy has left the house. Woe is me. I'll lie here and wait for him to get back. Hopefully it won't be too long."

Really, is there anything more frustrating than waiting? Who loves a long grocery store checkout line? No one, but at least you can look ahead and see how many people are ahead of you, and with how many items, and you can approximate the length of the wait. But then you see the cashier pick up the little microphone and hear her announce, "I need a price check on Aisle 4." Good grief! But what's much worse is when you don't know how long the wait will be. You go to the doctor's office for an appointment. The nurse comes in, takes your blood pressure, and asks, "So, why are you here today?" First of all, she doesn't even know?! This is disconcerting in and of itself. And then she tells you that the doctor will be in, "shortly," leaves, and closes the door. And you wait, and wait, and wait. Ten minutes go by, and you think, "This has been a long time. I need to use the bathroom, but I'll wait because the doctor should be opening the door any minute now." Forty-five minutes later, you're still in that tiny little room, without hearing a word from the outside, and your bladder's about to burst. Couldn't someone have shown just a little empathy and opened the door to tell you approximately *when* to expect the doctor? Apparently, the word "shortly" means vastly different things to different people.

When I leave my house, I am sensitive enough to my dog's feelings to tell him about how long I'll be gone. "I'll be back in about an hour, buddy. Just going to the store." Or sometimes, apologetically, "It's going to be a while, buddy. Sorry. I'm going to miss you too. Kisses." And then before shutting the door I give him one last look, and I see those big, brown eyes downcast, with a look of hurt and betrayal on his face. "Daddy, how could you possibly leave me? I'm miserable without you."

As much as I'd like to pretend that my dog understands every word I say—and truth be told, he understands a whole lot—I really don't think that he has the capacity to understand my communication with regard to how long I'll be gone. Maybe my tone of voice gives him some clue, but by and large he is left to wait, alone, not knowing when Daddy's coming home. I've been left alone in the doctor's office. Alone, waiting, expecting, waiting. I know what he's going through. And I hate doing it to him.

How do you think God feels about waiting? Well, since God does not experience time in a linear fashion like us, I'm not sure if we can really say that God "waits" for anything. From our perspective, He is patient with us, and for that we should be thankful. But just because God exists on a different plane of existence doesn't mean that He doesn't understand how we feel when we are waiting. Jesus lived a fully human life, and I'm sure that it involved plenty of times of waiting. Waiting in lines, waiting for food, waiting for His time to reveal Himself, waiting for His thick-headed disciples to get it! There's nothing in this life that we experience with which God cannot empathize, since God lived it all like us. He stepped into time, clothed Himself in human flesh, and experienced time first-hand from a human perspective. That's not to say that He couldn't understand it before—I'm sure He could—but it's comforting to know that He experienced it as well. Waiting is never fun, but it is reassuring to know that we have a God who understands.

"But do not ignore this one fact, beloved, that with the Lord one day is like a thousand years, and a thousand years are like one day. The Lord is not slow about his promise, as some think of slowness, but is patient with you, not wanting any to perish, but all to come to repentance." — 2 Peter 3:8-9 (NRSV)

- How does your dog behave when he is left alone in the house?

- Put yourself in your dog's shoes…err, paws for a moment. Your beloved master has shut the door and you have heard him start the car and drive away. You have no idea when he'll be back. How does this make you feel?

- When is the last time that you were waiting for something, not knowing precisely how long it would be? Were you patient? Hopeful? Irritated? Distressed?

- What are you waiting for now? A package to arrive in the mail? A response to an e-mail? Healing from God?

- How does knowing that Jesus experienced these things help you to deal with these times of waiting?

*Dear Lord, if patience is a fruit of the Spirit, please enable that fruit to grow. Waiting can be a painstaking endeavor, especially when I don't know how long it will take. Whatever it is, I trust that You know all these things, and that, by Your Spirit, You would enable me to trust in Your provision as I wait. They say, "Patience is a virtue," and, "Good things come to those who wait." Yet my hope is not in the mere passing of time, but in Your proven faithfulness. Help me through these difficult times of waiting, Lord, and set my heart and hope expectantly upon You, I pray. In Jesus' name. Amen.*

# 48 Appreciation

Most of these devotional thoughts have centered around the idea that the way we relate to our dogs provides us with some understanding of how God relates to us. Today's reading, though, is a little different. It references a rather traumatic event that took place when Jedidiah was ten years old, and this entry was written about two weeks afterward. Simply put, it is a call to appreciate the dog in your life and give thanks to God for forming this "holy union," as it were.

As an older dog, Jedidiah has nevertheless acted like an energetic puppy most of the time. Even at ten years of age, He still has a very young face, and when people ask how old he is, they are genuinely shocked to hear that he's older than three or four years. His age does become apparent late at night when he acts like a grumpy old man at bedtime, though, for the most part, he does not act his age. But after a recent routine visit to the vet, it was as though he went from being a young pup to an octogenarian knocking on death's door in an instant. He had been sedated for his exam, vaccinations, and nail-clipping. However, upon reversal of the sedation, it was as though the back part of his body never woke up. He could not put any weight whatsoever on his back legs and had to be carried out to our car. I monitored him closely over the next twenty-four hours and stayed in touch with the vet, thinking that, for some unknown reason, it was just taking longer than usual for the effects of the sedation to wear off. But it became apparent that something else was wrong because he was now experiencing a lot of pain in his rear extremities. With every step, he cringed, arching his lower back. At one point, he tried going upstairs but got himself stuck on the third step, unable to raise himself or turn around. He ended up tumbling down backwards. He could not even bring himself to sit because the motion of getting into a sitting position was too painful to attempt. The second night after his vet visit, he paced in circles, panting, until 4:48 a.m., when I finally coaxed him into lying down on a mattress that I had laid out on the floor. And getting himself back up was just as painful. In just two days, he had gone from his usual energetic, happy self to a dog that looked as though his days were numbered.

Very concerned, our vet got us an emergency appointment with a veterinary neurologist an hour and a half away. The neurologist took a look at Jedidiah's gait and concluded that he was likely experiencing a slipped vertebral disc in the lower lumbar-sacral area. If correct, the disc was pushing on some nerves and causing pain to his rear extremities. The neurologist prescribed medication to alleviate the nerve pain and reduce inflammation. As a result, Jed improved remarkably over the next few days, and was soon back to walking without any sign of pain. Slowly but surely, he began to regain some of his more usual behaviors, although we were careful to limit his activity. He literally went from being completely normal, to looking as though he was on the brink of death, and then back to regaining his form in less than two weeks.

During this crisis, I spent a lot of time reflecting and simply appreciating Jedidiah for who he is. The healing came through medication and much prayer. It would be pointless to try to estimate how much of his recovery could be attributed to God's healing and how much to the medicine, as if it could be charted. I simply thank God and praise Him for Jed's healing, and continue to pray for complete recovery, since he's not 100% back to his old self yet. Or "young self," I should say. He hasn't yet grabbed a toy and asked to play tug-of-war. But even if that never happens, there is so much for which to be thankful. Now I see Jed walking like a normal dog, without pain, and I thank God for that. I see him sit down and get up, and I'm thankful for that. As I pulled into the driveway on my way home from church this morning, I heard him excitedly barking from inside the house as he joyously welcomed me home, and I thanked God for that. These behaviors made me smile before, but mostly it was the status quo, and it is how I expected things to be. But now, after emerging from this life-threatening scare, in which we faced the possibility of Jed's passing, or perhaps worse—living in constant pain, and my wife and I having to make difficult end-of-life decisions for him—I am consciously thankful for the "normal" of my dog's life.

So I encourage you to learn from our experience, without having to go through it yourself, to let this message sink in. Be thankful for your dog. Thank God that he sleeps. Thank God that he walks. Thank God that he looks at you with love. Thank God that he can go outside to do his business. Thank God for his health and well-being. God is the author and sustainer of life. One of my prayers when Jedidiah was sick was that God would heal him on the basis of His love because, after all, his name means "loved by the Lord." Of course, God loves you too, as well as your dog, whatever you and him are named. And on the basis of God's unfathomable love, we can come to Him for anything, and He calls us to pray in all circumstances. So I encourage you to take a moment and thank God for your dog, and appreciate everything about him.

Thankfully, Jed went on to make a full recovery.

**"Rejoice always, pray continually, give thanks in all circumstances; for this is God's will for you in Christ Jesus." — 1 Thessalonians 5:16-18 (NIV)**

- Have you ever had a life-or-death scare involving your dog's health?

- When was the last time you thanked God for just the "normal" of your dog's life?

- List some of your dog's normal behaviors, and thank God for each and every one of them.

- Throughout the rest of the day, try to be conscious of your appreciation for your dog. And thank God with a little "under your breath" prayer every time you're reminded of how blessed you are to have him in your life.

*Dear Lord, I want to take this moment to tell You that I appreciate my dog, and I appreciate You for bringing us together. I appreciate Your life-giving Spirit and Your life-sustaining breath. Nothing on this planet could survive without You, and that includes my dog. You fashioned him and You united us in a holy bond of love, and I am thankful for that. Thank You for every moment that I am blessed to spend in his presence. Truly, Lord, I have been blessed. I appreciate it, and I thank You for this treasured gift. In Jesus' name. Amen.*

# 49 The Walk and the Journey

Is there a dog on the planet that doesn't get excited to go for a walk? Think about your dog's daily routine for a minute. Sleep, sleep, sleep, greet my master, lie down, eat, go outside to potty, sleep, sleep, walk to another room, lie down, sleep. It can be pretty monotonous. So the minute your dog sees the familiar sight of that leash, it's no wonder that it's, "Oh boy, oh boy, oh boy! Let's go, let's go, let's go!" A leash means outdoors. A leash means time with his master. A leash means stimuli. A leash means adventure.

Although people will go for a hike in the woods simply to experience the peace and beauty of nature, most of the time when we leave our houses, it is with the express intent of going somewhere. We have an actual destination. Whether it's the store or someone's home or church, we go there in order to be there for some reason, and when we leave, it is to return home. There is purpose in the destination. But when we take our dogs for a walk, there usually is no destination. It's a round trip. The purpose is not *getting* anywhere; the purpose is the walk itself. My dog spends most of his time lying down in the house, so for him, twenty or thirty minutes of mild exercise and stimulation is the highlight of his day. There's so much to sniff and see, and so many places to pee!

Perhaps it would help if we looked at our lives more like a dog looks at a walk. We tend to always have the future in mind. Thoughts of how we want to advance in our careers probably occupy an inordinate amount of brain space, and so much of our days is consumed by it. I believe that planning for tomorrow is a very good and worthwhile endeavor, but sometimes we can be so consumed by tomorrow that we forget that we're living in today. It is important to know where we are going, but in the process we mustn't forget where we are. For a dog, the walk is the thing in and of itself. What if we looked at our lives more as a journey, enjoying each day for what it holds, with less anxiety about the future? What if we pictured Jesus walking with us, taking joy as we pause to appreciate the beauty in which we are surrounded? Our days are filled with so many beautiful sights—if we would just stop and take the time to notice them. And let us indulge our other senses as well. Turn up the music and get lost in the sound of your favorite instrument, whether it be the violin or the steel guitar. And as you're doing so, use a breath to thank the Maker of this goodness.

Each and every life is a journey. There will be pain and heartache; there will also be sweetness and pleasure. But the point is not the destination. Sure, there are great and wonderful accomplishments that are worth pursuing along the way. But God created you primarily in order to share His love with you in relationship with Him. Is there anything that He needs you to do for Him? I mean, really needs? He's God, remember? He created the universe; He can do anything. But He has created free-willed beings in order to share His love with them, and receive love from them. Not pre-determined or coerced "love" (that's not love!), but true, genuine, relational love. The purpose of walking our dogs isn't to take them somewhere; it is to be with them as they experience life. So too, the purpose of our lives isn't necessarily to get somewhere, but to walk with God as we strive to better ourselves and the world around us. And all the time doing so in close communion with God. We may have a destination in mind, but along the way, let's enjoy the journey.

"Seek the Kingdom of God above all else, and live righteously, and he will give you everything you need. So don't worry about tomorrow, for tomorrow will bring its own worries. Today's trouble is enough for today." — Matthew 6:33-34 (NLT)

- How often do you pleasure your dog with a walk?

- How does your dog react when he sees you holding his leash?

- What do you think your dog enjoys most about taking a walk with you?

- If you were to picture yourself today, in everything you do and everywhere you go, as though you were walking with God, how different would your day be?

- How does thinking of life more as a journey, with worth in and of itself, regardless of the destination, make you feel?

- What is there today—sights, sounds, or other sensory perceptions—for which you can take a moment to appreciate and thank God?

*Dear Lord, sometimes I get so focused on the destination that I forget that the journey in getting there is meant to be enjoyed. Things may get difficult, time-consuming, and frustrating along the way, but there is always something in which to find pleasure. And I know that if I spend all my mental focus looking ahead, I will never be at peace and happy in the now. Please help me to slow down, look around, and find joy in today. And change my mindset so that I'll remember that, though I may have a destination in mind, I live in the now, and, with You, I get to enjoy the journey. In Jesus' name. Amen.*

# 50 Bragging

"I have the most wonderful dog ever. No, really." Does this sound arrogant? Conceited? Well, perhaps, depending upon how the statement is delivered. But depending upon the heart behind it, it could be a healthy position to take. I, for one, think that every husband *should* feel as though he has the best wife in the world, far superior to all others. And I think that wives should feel the same way about their husbands. It's not meant to be an actual competition, and it's not objective. It is a purely subjective comparison.

Surely you have heard many a dog owner brag about their pets like this. Perhaps you've done the same. More likely, though, you've refrained from saying these words to a fellow dog owner so as not to hurt his or her feelings. "You're dog really is very cute," you might think, "but that mutt can't hold a candle to my little guy." You're proud of your dog, and you should be. It's hard not to brag sometimes.

But do we have this same attitude about God? Remember, He's accomplished a few remarkable things, like, oh, I don't know…creating the universe and giving you life, just to name a few. And don't forget about the life and death of Jesus Christ. He is perfect, holy, and loves even the most unlovable person with an indescribably pure love. I mean, if we're tempted to brag about our dogs, why not brag about our God?

I know that I'm approaching the line of irreverence here in comparing one's dog to God, but I don't think that I'm crossing over it. I am not saying that just because the one (dog) is the other (God) spelled backwards necessarily implies anything. What I am trying to do is touch upon our natural instinct to brag about the things we love and cherish, and of which we are most proud—namely, our dogs—and apply that same notion to the One who is ultimately the most lovely and cherished, the One in whom we should be most proud. If you can brag about your favorite sports team's victory and if you can brag about your children's accomplishments, and if you can brag about your dog, why not brag about your God?

"Have you seen my God? Look around you. See all that? I mean, *everything*. It's my God who made it all. Look at that flower. Smell its fragrance. My God made that. Over there in the grass. Scurrying along with those big puffy cheeks and soft brown fur. What's that? It's Mr. Woodchuck. Where did he come from? Oh, my God, He made him. And look up on a clear night. Do you see all those stars? The moon? Oh, a shooting star…did you see that? That came from my God. Now, think back for a moment about all the good things that have ever happened in your life. Treasured childhood memories. Family vacations at the beach. Your favorite grandparent. They all came from my God. And all your hopes for the future? The dreams you've yet to realize? Yup, my God. He even paid the penalty for me when I was guilty of sinning before Him! How amazing! I have the most wonderful God ever!"

Oh, and my dog, and your dog, and all the wonderful four-legged puppsters out there. Who's idea was that? Yup, it's God. Brag about Him the next time someone is loving on your dog. I do it every time someone asks what my dog's name is. "His name is Jedidiah," I say. "He is loved by the Lord."

**"God has united you with Christ Jesus. For our benefit God made him to be wisdom itself. Christ made us right with God; he made us pure and holy, and he freed us from sin. Therefore, as the Scriptures say, 'If you want to boast, boast only about the Lord.'" — 1 Corinthians 1:30-31 (NLT)**

- Of your dog's many wonderful qualities, of which are you most proud?

- Who was the last person to whom you bragged about your dog? What did you say?

- What are some of God's qualities about which you, His child, could brag?

- What are some things God has done in your life about which you could brag?

- Next time the opportunity presents itself, will you be ready to brag about what an amazing God you have?

*Dear Lord, You are the most wonderful. My mind cannot comprehend Your goodness, and I cannot imagine You having any better qualities. I thank You for my dog, but much more so do I thank You for You. For Your greatness in who You are and for the love You show me. I am proud of You and I want to tell everyone just how great You are, so that they might know You as I do. May I exult in Your love for all the days of my life. In Jesus' name. Amen.*

## Notes

# About the Author

Steven D. Cole grew up on Long Island, in the harbor town of Northport, New York. He was introduced to Jesus as a freshman at the College of William and Mary through InterVarsity Christian Fellowship. There, he also met his wife, Banu. After earning a Bachelor of Arts in Religion in 2000, Steven pursued his education at Gordon-Conwell Theological Seminary, where he graduated with a Master of Arts in Religion in 2003. He then went on to earn a Juris Doctor from Regent University School of Law in 2009 and is currently an Associate Member of the Virginia State Bar.

Steven has served in multiple positions at several churches over the past twenty years, including Community Group Leader, Director of Community Groups, Teacher, Administrator, Media Booth Director, and Advisory Board Member, among others. In his spare time, Steven enjoys fishing, golfing, kayaking, softball, and ice hockey. Steven and Banu currently reside in Earlysville, Virginia, with their beloved Alaskan Malamute, Jedidiah. They faithfully attend and serve at Cornerstone Community Church in Charlottesville, Virginia.

Made in the USA
Las Vegas, NV
20 December 2021